THE COMPANY
THAT SOLVED
HEALTH CARE

"JOHN TORINUS is a national treasure. Every business can learn from what he did at Serigraph."

—REGINA E. HERZLINGER,
Nancy R. McPherson Professor of Business Administration
at the Harvard Business School, author of *Who Killed Health Care?*

———

"THE HEALTH CARE INDUSTRY is badly in need of new business models and systems thinking. *The Company That Solved Health Care* incorporates some of the best management disciplines as it proves health and health care costs can be improved dramatically at the ground level."

—PAUL O'NEILL,
former CEO of Alcoa and Secretary of the Treasury

———

"TORINUS HAS SOUGHT OUT the best innovators in Wisconsin for delivering more value in health care, and he put them to work at Serigraph. His company has proved that purchasers of health care can manage their costs and control their destiny far more effectively than 'command and control' government approaches. He has pushed the industry hard to improve, and it has helped us get better. His prescription is on the mark."

—STEVE BRENTON,
President, Wisconsin Hospital Association

———

"WHILE MUCH OF THE COUNTRY is focused on the attempts to reform health care in Washington, there is a revolution going on under their noses. This book describes the real-world revolution that is transforming health care into a cost-efficient, accountable system through empowering consumers. John Torinus is no dreamer. He shows us how his company has walked the walk and actually made it happen. This is must-reading for every employer who is concerned about staying in business in a difficult economy."

—GREG SCANDLEN,
Editor, *Consumer Power Report*

"MANITOWOC COUNTY took a page directly out of the innovations for managing health care costs spearheaded by John Torinus at Serigraph, and it worked. We convinced our non-represented employees and six employee bargaining units to work with us in making these changes, putting millions of dollars into the pockets of our four hundred employees while capturing significant savings for taxpayers. Consumer-driven health care changes EVERYTHING!"

—BOB ZIEGELBAUER,
Wisconsin State Representative (D)
and Manitowoc (WI) County Executive

"TORINUS HAS SUCCINCTLY CHRONICLED the remarkable success at Serigraph in controlling company health care costs. This story serves as evidence to U.S. employers and the government that it's possible to bend the health care expense curve. His prescription? Work with employees to help them become better consumers by providing price and quality data on doctors, hospitals, and prescription drugs so they can take responsibility for their own health, and by creating benefit incentives that encourage the right behaviors. This isn't academic theory. Torinus has made it work."

—JOHN TOUSSAINT,
CEO, ThedaCare Center for Healthcare Value

———

"PREVENTION, WELLNESS, and chronic disease management have to be foremost if the nation is going to dramatically improve health and significantly lower costs of care. Serigraph's business model proves those initiatives work in a very real way. The book is a must for every business as it deals with health care."

—TOMMY THOMPSON,
former Governor of Wisconsin and
Former U.S. Secretary of Health and Human Services

———

"ANYONE HOPING to sit quietly on the sidelines until John Torinus tires of his campaign to change health care in our country would do well to remember that John rode his bike across America at age 71 and skis through the hilly and frigid course of the American Birkebeiner. John brings the focus and energy of an endurance athlete to his work to keep his company competitive by changing the way we buy and, more importantly, think about health care.

Since I met John in 1996, he has been an active participant in health reform debates and a relentless voice for change. We were at the table together when a small group of Wisconsin providers

BenBella Books, Inc.
10030 N. Central Expressway, Suite 400
Dallas, TX 75231
www.benbellabooks.com
Send feedback to feedback@benbellabooks.com

Printed in the United States of America
10 9 8 7 6 5 4 3 2

Library of Congress Cataloging-in-Publication Data is available for this title.
ISBN 978-1935618-19-5

Editing by Debbie Harmsen
Copyediting by Lisa Miller
Proofreading by Erica Lovett
Cover design by Ted Mauseth/MausethDesign
Text design and composition by John Reinhardt Book Design
Printed by Bang Printing

Distributed by Perseus Distribution
(www.perseusdistribution.com)

To place orders through Perseus Distribution:
Tel: 800-343-4499
Fax: 800-351-5073
E-mail: orderentry@perseusbooks.com

Significant discounts for bulk sales are available.
Please contact Glenn Yeffeth at glenn@benbellabooks.com or (214) 750-3628.

"SERIGRAPH'S FOCUS, organizational commitment, and collaboration with its health plan administrator, Anthem Blue Cross and Blue Shield, and providers of value in health care proves that there are innovative solutions for getting the hyperinflation in health care under control. It's not a blame game; it's about individual engagement, transparency, and effective management."

—Steve Martenet,
President of WellPoint Specialty Products and
Former President of Anthem Blue Cross and Blue Shield in Wisconsin

How Serigraph Dramatically Reduced Skyrocketing Costs
While Providing Better Care,
and How Every Company Can Do the Same

THE COMPANY
THAT SOLVED
HEALTH CARE

John Torinus Jr.

BENBELLA BOOKS, INC.

DALLAS, TEXAS

BenBella Books, Inc.
10030 N. Central Expressway, Suite 400
Dallas, TX 75231
www.benbellabooks.com
Send feedback to feedback@benbellabooks.com

Printed in the United States of America
10 9 8 7 6 5 4 3

Library of Congress Cataloging-in-Publication Data is available for this title.
ISBN 978-1935618-19-5

Editing by Debbie Harmsen
Copyediting by Lisa Miller
Proofreading by Erica Lovett
Cover design by Ted Mauseth/MausethDesign
Text design and composition by John Reinhardt Book Design
Printed by Bang Printing

Distributed by Perseus Distribution
(www.perseusdistribution.com)

To place orders through Perseus Distribution:
Tel: 800-343-4499
Fax: 800-351-5073
E-mail: orderentry@perseusbooks.com

Significant discounts for bulk sales are available.
Please contact Glenn Yeffeth at glenn@benbellabooks.com or (214) 750-3628.

Dedicated to the pioneers in the bottom-up reform of health care economics in the United States, including Linda Buntrock, Ellen Lidtke, Carol Eady, David Kracht, Scott Fuller, Jo Thompson, Regina Herzlinger, Jim Mueller, Len Quadracci, John Toussaint, and Jerry Frye, and to Kine Torinus, my beloved wife and most stern editor.

Contents

INTRODUCTION:
REAL REFORM OF HEALTH
CARE STILL TO COME

THE TOP-DOWN REFORMS of health care that barely made it through Congress will have little impact on my company.

The major thrust of the Democrat-driven legislation was to improve access for the uninsured. Their concoction was mostly about who's covered and who pays. In one dimension, the national reforms are a form of wealth redistribution from the well-off to those in need.

In stark contrast, the major issue for businesses at the ground level has been the costs that have relentlessly escalated for decades. That pattern of a doubling of costs every eight years justifies the term "hyper-inflation." It continued into 2010 with premium increases for businesses of at least 10 percent and often more than 20 percent.

So the challenge for private payers has been to get some kind of grip on out-of-control health care charges. Congress and President Obama paid scant attention to the cost side of the equation. Worse, most of the insurance reforms, such as eliminating pre-existing conditions and barring lifetime caps on coverage, will serve to raise premiums in insured plans.

This book is a story of the development of a business model that brings sanity back to the economic side of medicine. It is a road map for private payers.

Further, the lessons learned in the private sector contain answers for insolvent public programs like Medicare and Medicaid. Politics in America has become so polarized and so bought-and-paid-for by entrenched interests that meaningful congressional reform of the public sector's health programs has proved near impossible.

But large-scale change often starts small. Remember welfare reform? It started in two counties in Wisconsin and then spread across the nation and to other parts of the industrialized world.

Grassroots reforms can catch fire and prove more powerful than mandates from the mountaintop. That is because ground-level concepts and experiments are put to the test of reality. Do they work or don't they?

This book is about the innovations that have worked. The collection of these initiatives adds up to a new business model for the delivery and purchase of health care in America.

These ideas come none too soon. The healing side of medicine is usually caring and often brilliant. But the economic
side is breaking the bank at all levels of society: national and
state budgets, company profit-and-loss statements, and personal wallets. No less than the national solvency is at stake.

There's a huge irony in all of this. The reason access
became a major issue in the first place was that costs and
prices got so high that growing numbers of Americans
couldn't afford that access. Individuals and small companies dropped coverage because they couldn't afford it. The
higher the costs moved, the larger the uninsured population became.

The root cause of the problem has been ineffective cost
management. Unlike effective businesses, which try to find
and fix the root causes of problems, Congress has attacked
the symptoms. It turned a blind eye to the underlying cost
structure in the largest industry in America. It attempted
what Congress does best: toss more money at the problem.
Congress raised billions in new money through taxes and
cost-shifting to buy access for those who had been priced
out of coverage.

Most Americans would agree that covering the uninsured is the right thing to do. But most taxpayers wish
that Congress and the Obama administration would de-
vote more attention to the ways and means of paying for
universal access.

If our political leaders had listened to the pioneers in
health care delivery, the huge bill for universal coverage
could have been paid for with savings from better business

models. America is the citadel for business model innovation, and that talent is just as vigorous in health care as in other economic sectors.

Serigraph has sought out those new approaches and has put them to work to manage health and health care. The company has been a hothouse incubator for private sector reforms.

Not all have worked, but many of them have proved effective. They have driven down the cost enough that co-workers at Serigraph have seen only three small premium increases in the last seven years. The average increase in total medical costs for Serigraph and its co-workers has been 2.8 percent per year, far below the national average of 7 percent.

Serigraph co-workers deserve that premium relief because they have been full-fledged partners in making the company's new strategy work. Indeed, no human organization can succeed without the full engagement of the people in the system.

Therein lies the philosophical gulf between ObamaCare and Serigraph. The national legislation relies largely on mandates from Washington, D.C. In addition, recipients of the governmental largesse are essentially passive players. In one sense, people using entitlements become wards of the state.

In contrast, the private sector reforms rely on the intelligence and responsibility of the people receiving and purchasing care. Serigraph's reforms are at the grassroots level, not from the top down.

This book will take you along the learning journey that enabled Serigraph to tame the runaway beast of health care cost inflation. We have learned from many smart operators, some cited in this book. We continue to learn about promising developments in the incredibly complicated world of health care.

The potential improvements in human health and the potential cost savings remain enormous. They constitute gold-plated answers, and we will continue to mine them to offset future inflationary pressures.

For the sake of clarity, I have chosen to group the successful reforms in the private sector under three platforms:

- Consumer Responsibility
- Centers of Value
- Prime Role for Primary Care

CONSUMER RESPONSIBILITY

Companies that have used what are called consumer-driven health plans have enjoyed savings of 20–40 percent. That's because their employees have their own skin in the game. Behaviors change on a dime when companies give their people personal accounts that are tied to high deductibles and co-insurance. They become more personally responsible.

Employees act as if it were their money being spent on their health care, because it is. Over-utilization disappears;

utilization drops to appropriate levels. People shop around for value—the combination of better price, service, and quality. They take a sharpened interest in their own health.

This brand of reform has been proven to work over the past decade, and the savings are beyond debate. Yet the Democratic reformers shunned consumerism in their legislative gyrations, even as the number of high-deductible plans continued to grow rapidly and the savings mounted. Instead, the national reformers have opted for essentially free plans. They thankfully left personal health accounts largely alone.

Blank checks are usually costly, and most government programs that eschew incentives and disincentives are headed for fiscal crisis. That is not an exaggeration. The best-run public programs cost two to three times what cutting-edge private sector plans are paying.

Getting to consumer responsibility is not just about monetary incentives and disincentives. It's also about getting the right information in front of health plan members, such as comparative prices for treatments at area health providers. Think of what Travelocity does for airfare. Employers also need to disseminate quality ratings and reports on a broad range of medical treatments.

Communication and education must be clear, consistent, and easy to access.

Centers of Value

The second platform for reform helps people find the best providers. That means identifying and promoting what Serigraph calls "Centers of Value," where value means the best combination of service, quality, and price.

Most Americans have almost no idea whether their doctor or hospital system is good, bad, or average for performance. The information has been nearly impossible to track. In contrast, Serigraph makes available to its co-workers the quality ratings that are available. The performance variation is huge.

So is price variation. The same operation can vary in price by a factor of two to three times. We make such comparisons available on our intranet site.

We then set up rewards to steer our co-workers to the best-in-class providers. That includes providers outside our region and as far away as Bangalore, India. Huge savings result.

Some of these world-class medical providers are using the same lean disciplines that helped Asian carmakers ascend in the world of automobile manufacturing. By emulating their high-quality, low-price model, lean medical centers have eliminated thousands of errors and cut millions of dollars in costs. Their prices reflect their lower cost structures. (Toyota's problems in 2010 resulted from a retreat from those disciplines.)

There is even a moral ingredient to using the best doctors and hospitals. How can we justify benign neglect and condone an under-informed selection of sub-par providers by our people?

PRIME ROLE FOR PRIMARY CARE

The third reform platform is a model that centers on primary care, a little like it was in the good old days when doctors and patients had a personal relationship, both for care and for the economics of care.

A large swath of costs can be cut by re-establishing the role of primary care. Big, complex medical systems have homed in on the higher reimbursements offered by the government and insurance companies for specialty care. They put high-priced specialists at center stage.

As a business strategy, the big corporations have hired or acquired primary care physicians to feed patients upstream to their monstrously expensive specialty units.

The cost meters run wild when a specialist sends a patient to a hospital. An overnight stay in the best hotels in the world goes for $1,000 to $1,500. An overnight stay in an average hospital can run $5,000.

Further, care in these complex organizations invariably becomes fragmented and piecemeal. People are fixed for their symptom of the moment and sent home.

Companies that have brought primary care back into the forefront have cut their health budgets by as much as one-third below national averages. Often they have doctors, nurse practitioners, and nurses on site.

Such primary health care is more intimate and more integrated. Prevention, wellness, and chronic disease management become personal, proactive, and real, instead of a token effort on a Web site or brochure. The primary providers collaborate with their patients and keep them out of hospitals, and the savings accumulate.

These three platforms could have been woven into the national reforms, but only small bites were taken of each. That omission notwithstanding, the private sector reforms are so powerful that they inevitably will be baked into future reforms in both the private and public sectors.

The savings will be needed, because many employers will continue to offer coverage to stay competitive for the best talent. However, no one can accurately project how many will choose to pay the low fines for not offering coverage under ObamaCare, in effect defaulting to government plans.

Those who continue coverage will need to learn to play the health care game better, because the hyper-inflation continues.

The following chapters will walk the reader through the grassroots initiatives of Serigraph and other innovators as they developed these better business models for health care delivery in America. Readers will get a first-hand look at reform from the bottom up.

Co-workers from Serigraph help to tell the story through their experiences in seeking value in health care. (These fellow reformers have all given permission to cite their examples.)

It has been a rewarding, exciting journey for Serigraph and its engaged people. We hope you will put these powerful innovations to work in your organizations.

Rampant Health Costs
Can Be Controlled

I N 2003, I came to the realization that wildly out-of-control health costs could take down my company. We ended that year with a total health care bill of $5.5 million for employer and employees combined, up almost 12 percent from 2002 and 23 percent from 2001.

Further, we were looking at a 15 percent hike in 2004, an increase of more than $800,000. We had other expenses under control, but our health costs were metastasizing. We could not afford hyper-inflation in this major cost bucket. We had to do something about it and do it fast.

Serigraph is a mid-sized company that sells graphic parts, like the face of your car's instrument cluster. We sell to major consumer products manufacturers. We are two layers down the supply chain. So we lack leverage and are unable to pass on cost increases through higher prices.

Worse, our reality is heavy pressure to lower our prices each year of a multi-year contract. These "price-downs" mean we live in a world of deflation. We have to match the "China price" or the "India price" through high productivity and cost control. That makes us particularly vulnerable to hyper-inflation in any major cost sector.

Health costs are our third-largest expense after payroll and raw materials, and in 2003 they were heading to second-largest. We had no choice but to tame this runaway beast. Gaining control of medical expenditures had literally become a matter of survival for our manufacturing operations in the United States.

We had tried all the obvious tactics to lower health costs. Those included a wellness and fitness program; an annual quoting and bidding process to land a percentage point or two more in discounts from health providers; some rationing (only one Viagra pill per week, for example), and a standard plan that shifted some costs to co-workers with a deductible of $300 and 20 percent co-insurance. These anemic attempts throughout the 1990s may have mitigated the rate of increase, but at the end of each year, we still showed staggering cost hikes.

Several alarmed CEOs and I had formed a coalition of sixteen major employers in Washington County, Wisconsin, where my business is located, to aggregate more buying power. With 18,000 lives combined as leverage, we negotiated hard and won a few percentage points of better discounts from hospitals, clinics, and doctors. Nonetheless, our costs kept escalating all through the decade, and a couple months of health care inflation wiped out the wins on improved discounts. Trying to use our buying power against the larger selling power of increasingly consolidated providers did not work. It was very frustrating. We seemed powerless.

Litany of Excuses

I went to dozens of sessions on the economics of medicine, only to hear the rationale for why the rise in health costs was inevitable and unstoppable. I listened to the political dialogue at the state and federal levels and came to the realization that most experts endlessly stated the obvious: health costs were rising fast and were taking an economic toll on everyone. They talked mostly about who would or should pay for the escalating costs, not about controlling them. That remains largely the case. Meanwhile, more and more Americans were being priced out of health care coverage.

The litany of excuses for relentless health cost inflation sounds like this:

- The population is graying, and that means more medical conditions.
- Trial lawyers have caused a litigious environment that necessitates defensive and unnecessary medicine.
- New technology, which drives costs down in most industries, drives up costs in health care.
- Medicare and Medicaid under-pay providers, who are then forced to shift costs to payers in the private sector.
- Insurers and their executives make too much money.
- Doctors make too much money.
- Hospitals and their executives, including nonprofits, make too much money.
- Shortages of medical professionals drive up wages.
- Drug companies spend too much on advertising.
- Hospital systems are required to do charity care.
- Americans are too fat, eat and drink too much, don't exercise enough, smoke too much, and don't follow treatment regimens.

Serigraph did not have the luxury of bowing to those excuses. We could not take a duck on the double-digit inflation. And I did not want to cost shift to my co-workers.

About that time, I discovered a book by Regina Herzlinger, a Harvard business professor, titled *Consumer-*

Driven Health Care. In it, she prescribed a strong dose of marketplace dynamics and employee empowerment, the kind of breakthrough thinking we had been seeking.

Her ideas made a lot of sense, especially since Serigraph had a long tradition of asking its co-workers to fully engage in solutions to complex problems. We have always said to our people: "Help run the company." They pitched in when we moved to total quality management. They bought in when we set a goal of customer intimacy. They took ownership of the results when we launched a lean journey. So why wouldn't they help with taming health costs—if we gave them the right incentives and tools?

Besides, individual responsibility is the American way.

A handful of pioneer companies had already embarked on consumer-driven options a year or two earlier and were reporting success. Humana, a large national health insurer, took the leap with its own people as guinea pigs. It reported a less than 5 percent cost increase for its own employees in 2003. That was a lot better than the double-digit inflation we and the rest of the country were experiencing.

We needed triage, so we moved fast. We took the plunge to a consumer-driven health plan on January 1, 2004. The decision carried considerable business risk.

We had to invest money up front—about $2,300 per family or $2 million company-wide—on the bet that consumerism and empowerment would save that much and more during the upcoming year. We were uncertain of the outcome and nervous about the up-front payouts to co-workers. At the heart of it, the gamble was that those new costs would be more than offset not only by the higher deductibles and co-insurance but also by individual behavior changes. We were hoping for improvements in utilization, purchasing, lifestyles, and improved personal regimens for dealing with chronic diseases.

Further, we decided to not just rely on incentives and disincentives but to offer a holistic approach to keep our people healthy and out of the hospital. That was based on the obvious premise that managing health and health costs must be done concurrently.

It did not take long to see that the reform was taking hold. Our people started shopping for better value in terms of quality and price. They started asking their doctors and clinics what treatments were going to cost. Most providers responded, "What do you care? Your insurance covers it."

Our people replied, "No, it's our money, too."

Total costs for 2004, including our up-front incentives, dropped—repeat *dropped*. That outcome was far, far better than the 15 percent increase we had projected under the old plan. Consumer-driven health care reform was working. More than six years later, it is still working. (See Appendix for plan outline.)

In 2003, Serigraph's medical costs averaged $8,302 per family. Health insurer Kaiser Permanente calculates the U.S. average each year and put it at $9,068 per family, so we were running 8.5 percent lower than the national average. In 2009, Kaiser put the U.S. average at $13,591. We came in at $8,631 per family, 36 percent below the national

EXHIBIT 1–1

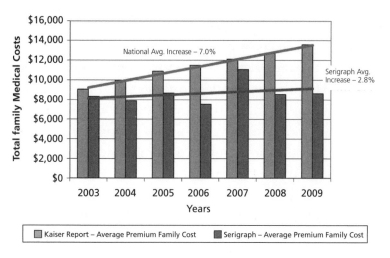

Serigraph Health Care Cost Trend vs National Trend

average (see Exhibit 1–1). The gap has grown wider and wider.

Serigraph and its people made that happen and learned many lessons along the way. We also learned from innovations at vanguard companies that have informed our health care journey.

Our hope is that our experience will encourage other companies and organizations to empower their employees as informed consumers and responsible patients. If enough payers do so, order will emerge from the chaos in the form of individual responsibility and marketplace disciplines.

Since Serigraph spends about one-third less than the national average for health care per employee, we save more than $1.5 million per year.

Let's extrapolate those savings. The annual national health care bill is $2.4 trillion, so a one-third reduction would save Americans $800 billion per year. That is enough savings to cover the uninsured in this country many times over. What has taken place on the ground level in our pilot program and elsewhere has major implications for the national health care policy. Ours is a ground-level solution rather than a stratospheric prescription from Washington.

Lastly, I would make a class-action apology for all CEOs. We allowed the mess on the economic side of health care to happen. We did not use the "Golden Rule"—he who has the gold rules. We are the payers, and we let loose the beast of hyper-inflation in health care. We did not trust and empower people to help. We did not put incentives and disincentives into place. We did not create a marketplace, the best form of price discipline. In the absence of strong leadership from business, we defaulted to government to take the lead on pricing policy and procedures.

I have been embarrassed for all of us who should have been in charge. But no more. Many private executives are no longer passive victims and complainants. Instead, we are beginning to manage our health care bills aggressively. Our hope is that Serigraph's journey toward proactive management of health costs provides a useful road map for others seeking to join us in taming the beast.

2

GET EMPLOYEES' HEADS
IN THE GAME

I KNEW WE WERE STARTING to win the battle against runaway health costs in 2004 when Serigraph employee Robin Reis came into my office incensed at what a local clinic would have charged for the removal of a small mole on his nose.

Before Serigraph converted to a consumer-driven health plan, he never would have asked the price. But because he had voluntarily selected a version of our health care plan with a $1,000 deductible and 30 percent co-insurance, he asked.

Predictably, the doctor did not know the answer. But Robin persisted. He elicited the list price for the forty-five-minute procedure, and he was flabbergasted. It retailed at $8,900!

Instead of passively accepting the quote, he decided to do some shopping. Another plastic surgeon, thirty minutes away, quoted $565 for removing the mole under a local versus general anesthetic. Robin would have to go back for a second procedure if the removed tissue appeared suspicious for cancer. That proved to be the case, so he had a second $565 procedure to remove the rest of the suspect tissue. It was successful, so the final bill came to $1,130. That was still a savings of $7,770. Because Serigraph is self-insured and pools and shares health costs on a 75/25 percent split with its co-workers, Robin helped us all. He saved money because his co-insurance charge was lower, the company saved, and Robin's fellow workers saved, too, because of the lower shared cost.

By 2010, six years into the new plan, annual premium savings per co-worker have grown to $1,250 from where they would have been had we not converted from our old health plan.

He recounted the outcomes, medical and economic, to his primary care doctor at the local clinic, and the surprised doctor responded, "You moved the business? Your company is one of our biggest customers."

In that instant, the marketplace started to work. Moving business, or threatening to move business, as anyone in business knows full well, often produces amazingly positive responses in a vendor.

Robin's example captures much of what needs to happen for health care delivery to become affordable, not only for Serigraph, but for the country.

What we have learned is that the winning formula for moderating health cost inflation comes down to:

- behavior change by individually responsible users of health care;
- aggressive and intelligent management by the company;
- creation of marketplace dynamics to help people find good value; and
- keeping people out of hospitals.

A WINNING FORMULA

Think of the winning formula in Robin's case:

First and foremost, Robin's behavior changed. He acted like a responsible individual, as he does in other parts of his life. He took charge. He behaved like an intelligent consumer and performed like an engaged co-worker. He helped not only his own wallet but also the company's treasury and its competitiveness.

Second, it was the first time this provider had *ever* referred to my company as a "customer." Because we are self-insured, we pay most of the medical bills. Usually the payer in any rational economic system is regarded by the payee as a customer. Only in health care is this not the case because we rely on the middleman, the third-party insurer, or administrator to pay the bills.

Third, the lack of concern about prices on the part of most providers was laid bare. They charge whatever they want because there is generally little discipline to require them to do otherwise. There is neither marketplace competition nor effective government regulation.

Fourth, a small piece of transparency came into play. Robin insisted that he be provided with a price estimate, much as if he were buying a car, a house, or a refrigerator. Ideally, he would have been able to view comparative prices for a mole removal at all area facilities. Ideally, those prices would be a bundled price for the complete procedure. There wouldn't be added charges for anesthesia, radiology, lab work, etc. The bill would show one inclusive total, clinic and doctor charges combined, net of discounts. It would be a bundled versus unbundled price.

Ideally, Robin should have been able to view comparative quality as well. Data on health care quality was not available in 2004; that information is just starting to appear.

Fifth, in this one small transaction, the market dynamic worked in health care. If everyone behaved like Robin, order would emerge from the chaos in health economics. If millions of consumers demanded better value from health care providers, broad reform would happen in short order at the grassroots level. A tipping point would be reached. The providers would have to compete on value: the combination of service, price, and quality. All providers would have to move to the lower price point to compete and stay in business. The $8,900 price originally quoted Robin would be history (see Exhibit 2–1).

Providers now compete on the number and size of their edifices, on technology breakthroughs that may or may not advance the cause of good medicine, and on the profiles of their specialists. Do we need 128-slice scanners when most doctors say they haven't figured out how to get full measure from 64-slice machines? The expensive scanners make sense for research but not for clinical practice.

The health care companies use billboard advertising that stresses the service component of value but never the price component and only indirectly the quality ratings.

Typically the big health systems consolidate selling power by buying competitors, so they can enjoy the benefits of lessened competition. In big parts of Wisconsin, there is either a monopoly or duopoly. In the Milwaukee area, there are only four main providers. Few independent operators remain. Innovative start-ups, such as the Heart Hospital of Milwaukee, are often bought out or crushed by the big systems, which shut down referrals to new entrants. In the face of that kind of selling power, how do reformers have a chance?

EXHIBIT 2-1

MORE ON ROBIN'S CASE

Here is the nitty-gritty of how we convinced Robin and our other employees and their families to change their behaviors. We converted on January 1, 2004, to what is called "consumer-driven" or "market-driven" health care.

Our old plan used a standard deductible of $300 and a standard percentage for co-insurance of 20%. Both were so low that they caused little, if any, behavior change. Employees were disengaged.

If Robin, for instance, had paid an undiscounted $8,900 for his carcinoma procedure, he would have paid the $300 out of his pocket and $1,720 (20% x $8,600) as his co-insurance. The company would have paid the rest: $6,880.

Instead, he voluntarily chose a new plan and, in doing so, put his personal funds and his head into the game. We lowered his premium by about $1,500 to almost nothing and gave him $780 in a personal health account called an HRA (Health Reimbursement Account). It is similar to an HSA (Health Savings Account).

So he saved $1,500 from the get-go, and had $780 in new dollars to spend. In exchange, he accepted a higher deductible of $1,000 per person and a 30% co-insurance level.

Assuming Robin had not shopped, under the new plan his billing of $8,900 would have worked like this: He would pay the deductible of $1,000 and 30% co-insurance on the balance (.30 x 7,900), or $2,370. His total would have been $3,370. He would have used his HRA of $780 for an adjusted bill of $2,590.

But because he now had money on the line, he shopped, and his bill looked like this: A deductible of $1,000 against a total charge of $1,130 and 30% co-insurance on the balance (.30 x $130), or $39. His total was $1,039. He could use his HRA of $780 for an adjusted bill of $259.

So, he personally saved more than $2,000 by shopping around. And, remember, he saved another $1,500 on his annual premium. (This run-down assumes this was Robin's first treatment of the year.)

On the company side, because Robin shopped his options, Serigraph saved more than $5,400—we would have paid $6,310 in the first scenario, whereas our portion came to just $871 in the second. The marketplace, consumerism, and competition saved both employee and employer a tidy sum.

Either government regulation or market-driven, bottom-up reform are the answers. I prefer the latter.

Reform starts with behavior change. That's never easy, as anyone who has tried to lose weight can attest. Serigraph had to have the courage to invest in up-front incentives and invite its employees to be partners in the solution (see Exhibit 2–2). Robin had to change from being entitled and passive to being responsible and proactive. He had to take control and make his own decision about where to go for treatment. Like most of us, he had been accustomed to following "doctor's orders." This time around, he had to tell his doctor he was going elsewhere for better value.

Private sector payers have learned that controlling costs is not about chasing a few more points of discount. That is what most employers did in the 1990s by pitting one health insurer against another through an annual bidding process—without much success. Double-digit inflation in health care costs persisted through most of the 1990s.

IT'S ALL ABOUT BEHAVIOR CHANGE

We have learned that keeping costs in check is all about behavior change. That is where the savings lie. Specifically, employees need to be asked to change five behaviors:

- how they utilize medical services;
- how they buy health care;
- how they live their lives in terms of personal health;

EXHIBIT 2-2

HIGHLIGHTS OF SERIGRAPH CONSUMER-DRIVEN HEALTH PLAN FOR 2010

- Self-insured with 1,200 lives covered
- High deductibles of $750, $1,000, or $1,500
- Co-insurance of 30% in network
- Low premiums, raised only three times by small amounts in seven years
- Health Reimbursement Account ranging from $468 to $3,120
- Flexible Spending Accounts available
- Maximum out-of-pocket for co-workers ranging from $3,250 to $6,000 per person in network
- Stop Loss of $200,000
- Free prevention for mammograms, Pap tests, prostate tests, colonoscopies
- Cheap doctor visits at $20
- Required annual mini-physicals, including blood work
- Up to two wellness days off for healthy lifestyles
- Rebates to co-workers of $250 to $2,000 for selecting from a panel of Centers of Value for different procedures
- Transparent price and quality ratings on company intranet site
- Biometrics for total population tracked for aggregate progress
- Only $5 co-pays on generic drugs; no co-pay if generic $1-per-week plans at Walgreen's, Walmart, or Target are used
- Free on-site clinic, including nurse practitioner, nurse, dietician, and chiropractor (who advises on floor ergonomics)
- Free primary care through retainer doctor, who acts as "medical home"
- Access to personal health record in medical home
- Proactive management of chronic diseases, including coaching and incentives for following treatment regimens
- On-site fitness center and walking paths
- Free elective procedures under medical tourism program at high-quality hospitals in other states and abroad, offered at a bundled price

- how they follow regimens if they have a chronic disease; and
- how they relate to their doctors.

Robin changed how he purchased health care and drove thirty minutes for a better value. Harnessing such behavior change is a winning game plan toward ending hyper-inflation.

Most of the national debate, and subsequent legislation, is about access and cost-shifting either to employees or to other payers: the government, taxpayers in general, specific taxpayers, and/or consumers via passed-on taxes on health care vendors. But that does not reduce the national health care bill; it just shifts who pays. Behavior change accomplishes what cost-shifting does not.

At Serigraph, co-workers are doing their best to get a handle on the runaway costs. But they cannot do it without help. They need the incentives to make it worthwhile to rein in expenses. As we have journeyed down the reform road, we have tried even more cutting-edge practices, such as sharing savings on procedures directly with our co-workers through cash rebates or by giving them time off for healthy behavior. More about this later, but these kinds of incentives have worked.

Comprehensive, long-term reform requires employers and employees to work together to bring their total health care bill under control. Think about how many ways the employees come out ahead if they take responsibility for their health care behaviors:

- they eliminate or reduce annual premium increases;
- premiums stay lower than state or national averages;
- their co-insurance and co-pay levels are lower (once past their deductible);
- they keep the unused portion of their personal health account, and it rolls over to the next year;
- they are healthier and they stay out of hospitals, which are risky places;
- they get cash rewards for going to Centers of Value (more on these centers in Chapter 5);
- they can take advantage of free prevention and wellness programs, cheaper drug programs, and rebates for intelligent purchasing in well-designed plans;
- primary care can be free;
- some procedures and generic drugs are actually free;
- profit sharing and wage increases can be higher; and
- their job security is enhanced, because their company is more competitive.

Adding it all up, behavior change is a win all the way around for the company and co-workers. Further, it is hard to see how any reform can work at any level without individual responsibility. Effective organizations and systems require the full engagement of all participants to make good things happen.

Name_____

Address_____ Date_____

℞ TAKE-AWAYS FOR TAMING THE BEAST

☑ Give employees the right incentives to change their behaviors. It is all about behavior change.

☑ Trust and encourage employees to get their heads into the game of controlling costs.

☑ Go to a consumer-driven, high-deductible plan, offset by personal health accounts. Those plans unequivocally have been proven to work. Dump plans with no or low incentives and no disincentives.

☑ Forget about chasing discounts as a main strategy.

☑ Get co-workers to understand that they and the company need to work together to have a winning game plan on health and health costs.

☑ Savings flow to employees in multiple ways.

MD_____

Signature_____

3

Utilization Drops Sharply with Individual Responsibility

IN THE MIDDLE of my eighth physical therapy session following surgery to repair a torn quadriceps tendon, I thought, "Haven't I been here before?"

The answer was "Yes." The eighth session was an exact repeat of the sixth and seventh. The therapist, who had done excellent work rehabilitating my knee in the early sessions, was now only passively overseeing my workout. I was doing the drills on my own. He was doing paperwork.

Because I was in a consumer-driven health plan, I asked him how much he was charging. It was $60 per unit, he said. What is a unit? Fifteen minutes. So he was charging $240 per hour. Not bad pay, but the guy did have a master's degree. (That was back in 2004. By 2010, rates had more than doubled to $500 an hour!)

I started thinking about my deductible and the co-insurance. At that point, I thought I could do the exercises on my own. The therapist and my orthopedic surgeon agreed.

That decision saved me and the company a couple grand.

Such rational reductions in utilization were the most immediate impact of Serigraph's switch to a consumer-driven plan in 2004. A snapshot analysis after the first year in the plan showed a 17 percent drop in utilization.

As an example, Resa Wronski, a commercial artist at Serigraph, recently warned all her co-workers to avoid expensive ambulance rides whenever possible. Her husband was moved twenty miles by ambulance from one hospital to another. The bill was $1,250, and they paid half. He didn't need paramedic care, and Resa could have driven him for the cost of a gallon of gas.

Getting our people off a nearly free lunch—low deductibles, low co-insurance—for health care really helped. They began to think and act like the responsible consumers they are in other parts of their lives.

After six full years in Serigraph's consumer-driven plan, utilizations have remained low. In 2009, inpatient admissions were 23 percent below the norm in the country, outpatient hospital visits 23 percent below, physician visits 24 percent lower, and emergency room visits 39 percent lower.

In short, the drop in utilization to appropriate levels drops immediately once the right incentives are in place, and it stays there. This is enduring change.

In contrast, Medicaid patients in Wisconsin, who get free care, often call 911 and then requisition ambulances for trips to emergency rooms for minor illnesses. ER doctors are outraged by the costly abuse.

The heart of any well-run human system is individual responsibility. Without that underlying platform, no organization or system can work well.

It has been a long tenet of Serigraph to "demanage"—to put decision-making into the hands of the people doing the actual work in what we call natural work units. Those can, for example, be a manufacturing cell, a sales group or an accounting team. An organization is much more dynamic, responsive, creative, and effective if appropriate decisions are made in natural work units instead of from the top.

That philosophy applies especially to big initiatives like total quality management, customer intimacy, lean operations, and innovation.

We have learned that empowering our co-workers to help manage health costs also works. Give them the right tools and incentives, and they become intelligent decision-makers.

Sometimes we use disincentives, like an immediate co-pay of $100 for use of an emergency room when it's not a real emergency. But mostly we have used incentives.

John Gildersleeve, a manufacturing supervisor, jumped into our incentive plan with both feet. He competes every February in the American Birkebeiner, a hilly, thirty-two-mile cross-country ski race in northwestern Wisconsin, the skiing equivalent of the Boston Marathon. He is a fitness buff who works hard to avoid hospitals and doctors. He had zero utilization of health insurance for several years.

Accordingly, as an intelligent consumer, he opted for the highest deductible plan of our three options, $1,500. As an offset, his health reimbursement account (HRA) had grown to $6,562 by 2009. It's there for future medical bills.

In the case of Serigraph, there is a company HRA account in his name that he can draw against. We put cash in when an employee draws on the account. Other companies use an HSA, an account whose popularity is increasing in this country (see Exhibit 3–1). That device requires a company to put cash in a personal account for each employee, so it is a bigger up-front cash commitment.

HSAs are tax-free going in, tax-free on the build-up in the HSA investment, and tax-free going out if used for medical purposes.

Both HRAs and HSAs introduce responsibility into individual behavior, with positive effects on consumption of medical services. There were an estimated 20 million

EXHIBIT 3-1

HSA Growth

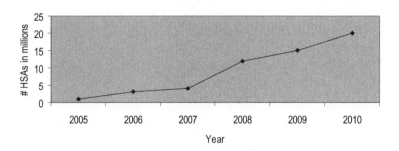

Year

Americans in HRAs and HSAs by early 2010, split about evenly.

Critics of high-deductible plans contend that they breed under-utilization of medicine. We have not experienced that at Serigraph. We believe, however, that over-utilization has mostly disappeared.

Besides, we make all prevention and wellness services free, and doctor office visits cheap at only $20. We want our people to consult their physicians early and often, before an illness becomes a problem.

In contrast, we have nearby examples of over-utilization. Our local school system, with whom we shared a database and network in the 1990s, has low deductibles, premiums, and co-insurance, and its employees used four times as much mental health care as the fifteen other local employers in the group. The stress of their jobs doesn't explain a four-fold difference. Because the benefits were virtually free, they were over-utilized.

In speeches on health care costs, I recount that when I was in the U.S. Marine Corps, Friday night happy hours featured ten-cent martinis. On occasion, I over-utilized. It is human nature to take advantage of near-free stuff.

Another criticism of consumer-centric health plans is that they are just a way of shifting costs from the company to employees. And, certainly, some companies have cost-shifted.

But they don't have to. We don't at Serigraph. We had a long compact with our employees that the company will pick up 75 percent of the annual health care bill, and the employee premium would cover the remaining 25 percent. That is about the national average for the employer/employee split.

We made it a fundamental principle when we went to the consumer-driven plan that we would maintain that split. It varies a little year to year, depending on occurrences. In 2008, it had moved to a cost sharing of 80 percent company and 20 percent co-workers. So Serigraph was picking up a bigger, not smaller, percentage of the tab.

The best news for Serigraph's co-workers is that we have raised premiums only three times in nine years through 2012 since restructuring our incentive programs. In 2010, our seventh year into consumer-driven concepts, we saw our third hike, about 8 percent. Our 2009 experience, on which 2010 premiums were set, was not good. However, that increase is still in sharp contrast to hyper-inflation of health care premiums elsewhere in Wisconsin and the United States. In Wisconsin for 2010, premiums increased as much as 17–35 percent for fully insured plans. Small businesses and their insurance brokers have confirmed those painful price hikes.

If anyone needs to be convinced about what kinds of health plans work, look at the employers who ought to know best—namely, health insurers and health care systems. They are in the medical game all day, every day as providers. But they are also users of the system with large work forces.

Humana's first-year success with its own employees in 2003 proved to be no fluke. Its annual increases through the decade continued at less than 5 percent per year.

Our instinct to follow Humana's lead paid off.

Not surprisingly, most major insurers and hospital systems have followed suit with their work forces. That's so telling.

OTHER EXAMPLES OF CONSUMERISM

If these companies that are experts in health care are believers in consumer-driven plans, shouldn't the rest of employers, private and public, get aboard the employee-empowered bus?

Indeed, that is what's happening across the land.

KI, a large furniture manufacturer in Green Bay, Wisconsin, made its consumer plan mandatory in 2006. When it employed a deductible of $2,500, offset by a $2,500 HSA, it saw an immediate, sharp drop in utilization and overall costs. KI has stayed about $2,000 below the state average costs per employee.

Tim Sullivan, CEO of Bucyrus International, a global manufacturer of mining equipment based in South Milwaukee, Wisconsin, convinced the Steelworkers Union in 2007 to go to a $2,500 deductible plan, offset by a personal health account. All employees, including Sullivan and the management team, are on the same plan. Immediately, its health cost inflation ceased. A Bucyrus union leader told me health costs dropped 22 percent.

In Manitowoc County, Wisconsin, Bob Ziegelbauer was aghast at the county's hike in premiums after he was elected county executive. Ziegelbauer knows numbers; he holds an MBA from Wharton. In 2007, he was looking at an Anthem Blue Cross and Blue Shield quote of $19,000 per employee, or roughly double that of private payers in the state.

He went to his three hundred employees, who were in seven different bargaining units, and asked them to consider a plan with a $1,500 deductible and $3,000 personal health account. The quote for that plan—with the same coverage and same network of providers—was $12,000 per employee. That is 40 percent lower.

Why would that be?

It is because the actuaries at Blue Cross know that behaviors change remarkably when people have "skin in the game," even if the personal health accounts were given to them. It becomes the employee's money. Primarily, it is intelligent self-rationing that kicks in.

That is the initial behavior improvement, but it is quickly followed by better purchasing behaviors, improved lifestyles, and regimens to keep chronic diseases under control.

Ziegelbauer got non-union employees and six of the seven units to go along and then shared about half of the savings with the employees. His 40 percent premium reduction squares with the national experience, where consumer-driven plans have shown premium reductions of 20–60 percent.

In the central part of Wisconsin, the North Central Alliance, a three-county organization of nursing home workers, had a similar experience. Its one thousand workers, low-paid members of the Service Employees International Union, had seen no raises for several years— not good when you are only slightly above minimum wage. Runaway health costs had crowded out raises.

The solution? It was a consumer-driven plan called "Get More" in 2007. Each worker got a debit card and health account to use against higher deductibles and co-insurance. The savings were 12 percent in year one, and the administrator decided to use the savings to give raises to the workers. They got another raise in 2008. The workers were elated.

HSA Total Keeps Growing

The number of personal health accounts has grown steadily in the United States since it was introduced in the late 1990s. The accounts grew from six million in 2007 to eight million by 2009. They will keep growing in number because they work.

The number of high-deductible health care plans is also growing. Estimates for 2009 showed that 23 percent of Americans under sixty-five now have high-deductible plans, and one-half of the individual market has gone there. That number has grown, because those plans produce behavior change. Therein lies their affordability.

Expect to see a flood of new HSA accounts in 2014 when the federal government's bill kicks in to mandate health insurance coverage. Some individuals will choose to pay the small fine and still go uninsured, but many will seek affordable coverage, and that often means a consumer-driven plan with a high deductible and offsetting health account.

And they work as soon as they're introduced. The large insurer Cigna released a report in early 2010 that showed costs dropping by 14 percent in the first year of a consumer-driven plan and accumulating to 26 percent in the fourth year as people become better consumers.

We have deduced that happens because people like being in control of their health care economics. They want the right to choose doctors and treatments. They want to make decisions on rationing for themselves, not have faceless bureaucrats do it for them.

They also deeply appreciate that the company is taking a huge interest in their health.

As a result, Serigraph's health plan ranked highest of all aspects of the company in an employee survey three years into our reforms. Our health plan has proved to be a morale booster and a recruiting and retention advantage.

Tammy Burdey, who joined the company two years ago as a credit analyst, takes advantage of our on-site dietician in order to keep her diabetic condition under control. She said Serigraph's plan is far superior to other places where she or her husband have worked. "I've *never* been healthier than since I've been involved with health care at Serigraph," she said.

An employee survey late in 2009 showed 220 of 370 respondents "always happy" with the Serigraph health plan, 138 "sometimes happy," and only twelve, or 3 percent, "never happy."

Most co-workers have come to think of the health plan as their plan. They own it, at least part of it. And they start to view their health as a personal asset.

Name

Address _____ Date _____

R̶x̶ TAKE-AWAYS ON UTILIZATION

☑ Utilization drops sharply with adoption of an employee-empowered plan.

☑ Cost-shifting is not the objective of a well-designed consumer-driven health plan.

☑ Savings flow to workers in multiple ways.

☑ Individual responsibility has to be built into any plan to attain cost control.

☑ Personal health accounts are popular with employees, who like to be in control of health dollars. They want the right to choose.

☑ Actuaries factor behavior change from consumer-driven plans into lower premium rates.

☑ People in consumer-driven plans come to think of the health plan as their plan.

☑ The higher the level of engagement, the better the plan works for improved health and lowering costs.

☑ The consumer-driven plan's incentives and disincentives are the catalyst for making all the elements of a health

MD strategy work effectively together.

Signature _____

Piercing the Fog
of Medical Pricing and
Promoting Transparency

J ILL HONECK AND SERIGRAPH overpaid for her husband's 2005 colonoscopy. Way overpaid. The gross charges were $13,000 for the inspection and removal of five polyps.

How do we at Serigraph know we overpaid when most consumers of health care have no clue about true costs? We know because we can compare prices.

Serigraph administers its health care through Anthem Blue Cross and Blue Shield, a large insurer owned by WellPoint, and together we made a huge leap in 2005 toward creating an open marketplace. We developed transparent prices for high-volume procedures across more than twenty providers in southeastern Wisconsin.

In 2009, Jill and her husband used our transparency model to choose a different provider for their colonoscopies. The gross charges were much lower at $2,472 and $2,797, respectively, and after discounts, net prices of $1,208 and $1,417.

By consulting our cost chart (see Exhibit 4–1), the Honecks saved the company thousands of dollars. The couple did such a good job of shopping that Serigraph picked up both of their deductibles and co-insurance. We made the preventive colon tests free, as we now do for all people in our plan who use a cost-effective colonoscopy provider.

Al Tackes, one of Serigraph's maintenance technicians, also had no problem driving outside the county to have a colonoscopy done at a cost-effective provider, the Milwaukee Endoscopy Center. He said the service and quality were excellent and the prices unbeatable.

This specialized facility has figured out how to deliver a routine colonoscopy for $1,127 and one with a biopsy for polyps for $1,250. That compares to sticker prices elsewhere as high as $11,000 for a colonoscopy with multiple biopsies for cancer testing.

EXHIBIT 4-1

MEDSAVE – Colonoscopy

The ranges are considered bundled prices.

The asterisk indicates facility/hospital is eligible for a rebate for this procedure. This facility/hospital combines a high number of procedures done with good discounted pricing.

Employees may choose any facility/hospital they prefer. Serigraph is not liable for the decisions made by the employee.

COLONOSCOPY 8/1/2009 — Rebate $500

Facility/Hospital	Address., Phone Number	Estimated cost	
Aurora Sheboygan Memorial Medical Center	2629 N. 7th Street 920-451-5000	$1577- $2028	*
Columbia St. Mary's Hospital (Milwaukee)	2323 N. Lake Dr. 414-291-1000	$1577- $2028	*
Froedtert Surgery Center	840 N 87th St. 414-805-9500	$1577- $2028	*
Menomonee Falls Ambulatory Center	W180N8045 Town Hall Rd. 262-250-0950	$1577- $2028	*
Milwaukee Endoscopy Center	8585 W. Forest Home Ave. #100 414-427-5138	$1127- $1577	Serigraph will pay 100% for using this facility
West Allis Memorial Hospital	8901 W. Lincoln Ave. 414-328-6000	$1127- $1577	*
Froedtert Hospital	9200 W. Wisconsin Ave. 414-805-3000	$2929 - $3380	
St. Mary Hospital Ozaukee	13111 N. Port Washington Rd. 262-243-7300	$2020 - $2480	
West Bend Surgery Center	1710 Vogt Dr. 262-334-6165	$2478 - $2929	

We were so desperate back in 2004 to pierce the fog of medical pricing that we took matters into our own hands. Linda Buntrock, our senior vice president of human resources, decided to use her MBA smarts to cut through the obfuscation. With some covert help from insiders, she came up with a Rube Goldberg pricing matrix on twenty-three procedures that account for a majority of the dollars spent on elective procedures.

Where no one else had prevailed against system-wide secrecy, Linda got it done. She posted her results on an intranet site for our co-workers, and, voilà, we had transparency. At least we had a start.

To get there, Linda had to fight off the clap-trap that the prices negotiated between the big provider groups and the big health plans were confidential. Included in their contracts was a clause that restricted either side from disclosing prices. What utter nonsense!

It may be their information, but it is also ours—we pay the bills, we write the checks. So, of course, we know the real prices. We, as one company with about twelve hundred lives covered, did not have as many data points on prices as a health insurer, but over time we could review enough procedures and bills to get to workable transparency.

In my view, consumers have an inalienable right to health care prices. After all, health care costs are so high that they knock some households into financial stress or even bankruptcy. Consumers have a need and a right to know up front what a procedure—especially a major procedure—will cost.

Beth Kreutzer, a customer service representative, echoed the experiences of most Serigraph people: "I have tried; it's almost impossible to get prices from providers."

Anthem Blue Cross and Blue Shield leaders agreed with us philosophically, that transparency is essential to creating a marketplace. So they quietly reviewed Linda's work and blessed her findings. They had many more data points than we did, so we could be assured what we were showing to our people was accurate and, further, that providers were being fairly represented.

The initial reaction of medical providers was to shrug off our transparency model. We were just one payer, and they could hide behind a Wizard of Oz curtain. A few, though, immediately asked what they could do to get into our best bracket. The market was moving a little.

About the same time, there were a few other moves toward transparency. The Wisconsin Hospital Association put out a site that listed "sticker prices" for hospital procedures. It included average discounts at each hospital. Their Web site was clunky to use, but it was an advance of sorts.

In 2008, Anthem Blue Cross and Blue Shield used its experience with Serigraph to roll out transparency nationally to a broad range of consumers.

Serigraph now uses Anthem's data as grist for our intranet pages, which shows pricing the most user-friendly way. Serigraph's transparency site includes twenty-seven of the highest-volume, most expensive procedures, such as a hip replacement (see Exhibit 4–2 for what Serigraph

EXHIBIT 4-2

Hip Replacement

The ranges are bundled pricing

The asterisk indicates facility/hospitals eligible for a rebate for this procedure. This facility/hospital combines a high number of procedures done with good discounted pricing.

Employees may choose any hospital they prefer. Serigraph is not liable for the decisions made by the employee.

Hip Replacement 8/1/2009 — **Rebate $2,000**

Facility/Hospital	# of Procedures/yr	Length of Stay	Overall Rating	Address, Phone Number	Estimated cost	
Aurora Sheboygan Memorial Medical Center	168	3.1 days	A	2629 N. 7th St. 920-451-5000	$18,000-$24,000	*
Columbia St. Mary's Hospital (Milwaukee)	63	4.2 days	A	2323 N. Lake Dr. 414-291-1000	$18,000-$24,000	*
St. Mary Hospital Ozaukee	96	4.4 days	C	13111 N. Port Washington Rd. 262-243-7300	$18,000-$24,000	*
Wheaton Franciscan Healthcare - Elmbrook Memorial (Brookfield)	153	4.3 days	A	19333 W. North Ave. 262-785-2000	$18,000-$24,000	*
India (Medical Tourism)				Arranged by Anthem	$10,000	Serigraph will pay 100% for choosing this option**
Community Memorial Hospital (Menomonee Falls)	197	4.0 days	B	W180N8085 Town Hall Rd. 262-257-3700	$34,500 - $39,800	
Waukesha Memorial	249	4.5 days	A	725 American Lane 262-928-2247	$23,900 - $39,800	

Overall ratings were found on Anthem's website

A = Scored in the top 25% of the hospitals overall

B = Scored in the middle 50% of the hospitals overall

C = Scored in the bottom 25% of the hospitals overall

** 100% coverage includes procedure, travel costs for patient and a companion, English-speaking 'concierge' to assist throughout stay, accommodations for the companion, post-op care and accommodations for patient prior to return trip home co-workers seeking price and quality information on a hip replacement find on our site). Among its other virtues:

- Doctor fees are included with hospital and clinic charges.
- Other line items that were unbundled before, such as anesthesiology, are included.
- Prices are shown for whole episodes of care, from beginning of treatment to the end, including physical therapy after surgery.
- Information on quality is added to identify what we call high-value providers. Some call them centers of excellence; we call them "Centers of Value." We steer our co-workers to those winners.

Combined with the Anthem transparency site, Serigraph can give good consumer information on 75 different procedures. This is just the kind of powerful information consumers need to make good choices.

CO-WORKERS OFTEN SEEK HELP

Serigraph's co-workers can use the company site on their own. However, more often than not, they come to the Human Resources office to get further counsel on how to navigate through the pricing minefield that characterizes the medical world.

During the difficult development of our transparent information, we held onto the tenet that patients have a right and the need to ask: "How much is this treatment going to cost?"

I asked that question about my pending hip replacement in 2005, before Serigraph rolled out its transparency model. The Web site at my hospital system of choice listed the charge before discounts at $27,000 for the hospital alone. When I called the hospital's 800-number hotline for more specific price information, the staff person guessed the price at $23,000.

I say "guessed" because when I asked if the prosthesis was included in the price, the person on the end of the line gave the hapless answer that he didn't know. When I asked the same question about anesthesiology, he didn't know. Pretty pathetic.

The most common response when a patient asks for a price is: "Why do you care? Insurance covers it." For a patient in a consumer-driven plan, that unresponsive comeback is unacceptable.

My hospital bill ended up at about $25,000 after discounts. It had twenty-two line items that neither I nor the chief financial officer at Serigraph could decipher. This is the confusing mess facing every health care consumer every day.

The surgeon billed $9,800, before discounts, for forty-five minutes of work on my hip. He is an excellent surgeon: fast, infection-free, good bedside manner. That's why I picked him after interviewing and checking out four other orthopedic surgeons. He does five hip replacements each Monday and Tuesday morning. You want a surgeon who does high volumes. He or she gets good at the craft. Higher volumes also show other doctors are referring cases. You don't want the doctor doing one a week.

He bills out at almost $50,000 each day. Not a bad morning's compensation.

RETAIL PRICES MEAN LITTLE

To show how meaningless retails prices are, my net price for the surgeon after discounts came in at $1,800. That is an 82 percent discount from the $9,800 sticker price. Only the uninsured face those horrendous "sticker" charges, because they are not connected to a network and the accompanying discounts. Some uninsured people succeed in negotiating a lower price prior to treatment, but many see their charges lowered only when they bargain with bill collectors.

Most provider discounts in the private sector are in the 20–30 percent range, but some are less and some are much more—depending, of course, on where some pricing guru in the provider system decides to set the retail price.

In near-monopoly areas, like northwestern Wisconsin, discounts are almost nonexistent. The providers can get away with high prices. One plan member broke an ankle skiing and received no discounts from the sole hospital in Ashland, Wisconsin. She was captive to their near-monopoly.

Adding to the pricing absurdity is the huge variation right within the sprawling consolidated health systems. The price swings from hospital to hospital—in the same system—can run two times from bottom to top. No one in our company, and not many in the region, knew that absurdity before the transparency efforts revealed the significant price differences.

In other economic sectors, politicians step in on the side of the consumer and mandate transparency. Car dealers, mortgage peddlers, and real estate agents are required by law to fully disclose every price item in a transaction. In a house closing, a buyer even has to sign a form saying he or she understands the full dimensions of the deal.

Transparency is required of stock brokers and mutual funds purveyors. Even car repair shops in Wisconsin have to provide an estimate, which the car owner signs. It is binding unless the customer is called and agrees to a higher charge.

Ironically, on the other end of a health care financial transaction, the medical providers want full information about your ability to pay. The first questions you are asked when you register are: "Do you have your insurance card with you?" "Are you still at this address?" "Do you carry any other health insurance?" They demand transparency about how they are going to get paid, but seldom reciprocate with transparency on how they are going to charge.

There ought to be a law.

Serigraph has repeatedly asked Wisconsin legislators and the governor to mandate price transparency, but nothing has happened. Nor has state government taken the easy step of making the prices it pays for coverage of its own employees transparent. That would provide at least one statewide portrayal of net prices.

It took until late 2009 for such a transparency bill to be introduced in Wisconsin.

Similarly, the national insurance reform falls short of requiring openness in prices.

Perversely, providers come after customers hard if they don't pay. Collection agencies, threats of legal action, credit impairment—all the hard tactics—are brought to bear. Little wonder health care bills are one of the leading causes of personal bankruptcy in the country.

Even when there is a legitimate dispute over a bill, the balance gets turned over to a credit agency, which promptly puts a black mark on a patient's credit rating. Removing the impairment means taking on an inert, impersonal, rules-driven bureaucracy. It takes months of determined effort.

OVERBILLING IS SYSTEMIC

Another part of the pricing opacity outrage is overbilling. It is systemic.

Brian Brodzeller, a Serigraph chemist, and his wife, Michelle, spent their Sundays poring over the huge, complex bill from the complicated premature birth of their daughter. They found a dozen mistakes, mainly for procedures that never happened.

Serigraph offers a reward for finding billing errors. It gives co-workers half of any recoveries. The Brodzellers didn't ask for the reward, but saved themselves and the company about one-tenth of the $100,000 bill. One charge was $6,000 for a procedure that never took place. Another $2,000 was a double billing. Ten more errors were for smaller amounts.

Brodzeller said he finds mistakes in every medical bill his family receives. "To be honest, you have to wonder if the many mistakes don't amount to fraud," he said. His bulldog approach succeeded more often than not in expunging the improper charges. But not every consumer of health care has that kind of tenacity.

Two years after the procedure, the Brodzellers are still trying to straighten out the mistakes in billing that won't go away. The bills aren't big enough for them to afford an attorney, so they fight the billing bureaucracies on their own.

There ought to be a law or at least some form of consumer protection.

In another instance at Serigraph, an employee was billed $6,000 for the removal of a bone spur from behind her Achilles tendon. Months later, she had exactly the same procedure done on her other ankle, and the price from the same surgeon, now in a new system, was $15,000.

She challenged the higher charge and was given no satis-faction. "The first one should have been billed higher" was the lame rationale.

Most medical overbillings and errors go largely unno-ticed in this country because the third-party payment sys-tem insulates the patient from most of the bill. Only when part of the payment comes out of a personal health account does the bill get the kind of scrutiny it deserves.

Rita Fellenz, wife of a Serigraph co-worker, was moti-vated by our cost-sharing arrangement to double-check her bills for a repaired rotator cuff. She was billed $5,472 for a room she never used in the outpatient procedure. The embarrassed hospital grudgingly expunged the item but never apologized.

She also called out the clinic on a $600 charge for a simple pre-operation physical. The bill was reduced to a more normal $300.

Not surprisingly, a niche industry has grown up in the United States that helps patients and companies root out mistakes. Auditing companies find errors in eight of every ten bills. Serigraph employs an outside auditor through Anthem for reviewing its major bills.

Most of the payment morass starts with the federal government. Tim Nixon, a retired sales representative for Serigraph, showed me his bill for cataract surgery. The gross charge for one eye was $3,688; Medicare paid a discounted $1,626, about 44 percent of the charge. Tim paid $50.

He didn't really look at the bill. At $50 out of his pocket, why should he? I pointed out that the bill contained five charges for "non-specific outpatient treatments" adding up to $1,724, almost half the bill. Those procedures weren't even coded.

That kind of unaccountable billing goes a long way toward explaining why Medicare is projected to go into the red in 2017, if not sooner. The mismanagement of prices starts at the top and sets a pattern for the whole country. The insurance industry, by and large, follows the Medicare pricing system.

Pricing in the non-market for health care is an opaque deck of cards. Nonetheless, we private payers still have to manage our way to acceptable results. We cannot use the dysfunction of the non-system as an excuse.

Serigraph continues to show its local providers where they rank poorly on price. They have moved slowly, but we are finally seeing some moderation in their prices. Without transparency, such progress toward accountability would have never happened. For a change, some prices are going down, not rapidly up.

In 2008, we added quality data to our matrix. Co-workers can come to the Human Resources Department to inquire not only about price but also about quality. That allows us to do a better job of steering our people to "Centers of Value." It's a win-win. The only losers are overpriced providers.

Five years after our transparency breakthrough, other big health insurers have been pushed or emboldened to put out their own transparency sites on prices. Finally, they are taking the side of the consumer and the payers like Serigraph. Anthem now publicly lists almost fifty procedures with bundled prices, including doctor charges. Humana has a similar site for one of its networks.

It's about time! Sunshine is finally piercing the unconscionable fog of medical pricing.

Name_____

Address_____ Date_____

℞ TAKE-AWAYS FOR PRICE TRANSPARENCY

- ☑ One way or another, get transparent pricing into the hands of employees.
- ☑ Encourage and educate co-workers on use of transparency sites.
- ☑ Guide co-workers through pricing maze to best deals, to "Centers of Value."
- ☑ Push politicians to mandate transparency as a consumer right.
- ☑ Push providers to offer bundled prices.
- ☑ Reward employees for finding billing errors.
- ☑ Push for consumer protection laws and regulations to remedy medical overbilling.

MD_____

Signature_____

5

Motivate Employees
to Seek Centers
of Value

ONCE THE CURTAIN is lifted on medical prices, you quickly learn that prices for various procedures vary wildly, often more than double from bottom to top. You learn that your company can steer people to the best deals.

In Milwaukee, you can pay as much as $35,000 in total for a new steel knee, or you can pay as little as $18,000.

Here are some other examples of the wide disparities in prices in southeastern Wisconsin:

	Low	High
Normal birth	$ 8,000	$12,000
Gall bladder removal	$ 3,000	$11,000
Caesarean birth	$12,000	$14,000
Spinal fusion	$30,000	$56,000
Heart catheterization	$ 4,000	$ 9,000
Knee arthroscopy	$10,000	$25,000

This chaotic pricing structure is typical throughout the United States and serves as an indictment on the economic side of American medicine. It suggests there is no discipline in what amounts to a non-system. There is neither a marketplace to force prices into line nor government regulators to contain prices. In other economic sectors, one of those constraints usually prevails. Health care is a no-man's-land.

In the absence of pricing discipline, payers like Serigraph have to try to create a semblance of a marketplace.

We decided to use carrots instead of sticks to motivate our co-workers to find the bargains. Our standard health plan features high deductibles and reasonable co-insurance, offset by lowered premiums and an HRA. The incentives motivate our people to pay attention to the craziness of medical pricing and to take advantage of the chaos.

While the consumer-driven plan won immediate positive results, we quickly spotted a major deficiency in our model. Most health plans, including high-deductible plans like ours, have a large flaw when it comes to major procedures. It's the out-of-pocket maximum for co-workers. Once a person hits $6,000 in out-of-pocket costs, Serigraph steps in to cover 100 percent of the remaining charges. It's back to free lunch and no consumer discipline.

Insights into this sinkhole came when I called Mike Heili, a friend and one of our long-time co-workers, after his hip replacement back in 2003. He was still in the hospital, and I asked him how it had gone. He said the surgery went well, and he couldn't wait to get out and get mobile again.

Then I asked him, "Mike, out of curiosity, how much did the operation cost?"

He responded, "I have no idea, John."

He got back to me a few days later, after asking, and said it would run between $50,000 and $60,000 before discounts, higher than normal, because it was a redo. Of course, therein lay the problem. Mike is a conscientious guy. He has always taken care of his own money, and he treated the company's like his own. He was beyond the out-of-pocket maximum, so he had no skin in the game. Why should he ask or care? He was just acting like a rational economic being.

Shame on us for not having the proper incentives and information in place so Mike could have helped us manage the costs. We were foolish back then not to exploit the huge price differences in the region to our advantage.

Cash Rebates for Good Buys

Our management dilemma was to keep people's heads in the game once they got past that $6,000 threshold. It came down to a choice of rewards or penalties. One Wisconsin company uses a stick; it doubles the out-of-pocket maximum if the employee doesn't go to a selected provider that offers good value.

Another stick approach we considered was to extend a small percentage of co-insurance above the $6,000 maximum, say 5 percent of bills above that threshold, to keep the employees in a consumer mode.

Instead, we decided to use the carrot approach: cash rewards if co-workers would go to the three or four providers we had selected as offering good quality, excellent service, and low prices. In short, we seek out good value, and we steer our co-workers to those Centers of Value.

We call our program MedSave.

After machine operator Jerry Minessale had his two artificial knees installed, he received a check from Serigraph for $4,000, or $2,000 per knee. The company gave him that cash reward because he used our MedSave program to search out a good deal on knee replacements.

MedSave works only for elective procedures, like Jerry's, when pre-planning time is possible. Emergencies obviously are not candidates for such rewards; they have to be dealt with at a nearby facility. But when there is time for pre-planning, it has worked well.

In the first five years, seventy-five co-workers directed their business to our Centers of Value. It has been a win-win for co-workers and the company. The co-workers have received checks for $55,000, and the company has saved more than $200,000.

If more companies steered rigorously to such centers, high-price providers would be forced to lower their uncompetitive prices or exit that line of work.

Our MedSave cash rewards range from $150 for an upper GI endoscopy to $2,000 for a heart bypass.

As might be expected, health care providers don't much like people shopping around in regional networks. They don't like people exploiting their pricing chaos. But they created the pricing jungle, so they don't have much standing to prevent consumers from using it to their advantage.

The wide range of prices occurs because the people doing the pricing know they are in a no-man's-land between marketplace and regulatory controls. In six years of researching solutions to high medical costs, pricing experts have repeatedly told me that hospital systems do little real cost accounting. They can price with virtual impunity.

That's so foreign from my manufacturing world, where costs are calculated several places to the right of the decimal point and then prices are set in some relationship to the underlying costs. Get too far away from a cost basis, and a manufacturer loses the work to a competitor.

That's just starting to happen in medicine.

In speeches on the subject, I point out to medical students that engineering students early in their studies are required to take a course in cost accounting. What good does it do to design a product that no one can afford?

I suggest to them that the Hippocratic Oath needs to be rewritten. It needs to be amended to say: First do no harm to patients medically but also do no harm financially. It is not ethical to bankrupt patients, their employers, or even governments with outrageous costs.

The word outrageous is justified. If one hospital can do a hip for $18,000, how can a nearby place justify $34,000? Why would or should anyone pay the higher price?

One legitimate rationale for patients going for a high-price solution is that they are comfortable with a long-time doctor. The confidence in that doctor may be justified, but it can be an expensive decision.

Most doctors have been consolidated into large health systems, and they are under huge pressure to send patients to specialists in their own corporations, regardless of price. Sometimes they earn financial incentives for doing so.

The other reason for not moving to best price might be "quality." Before throwing the red herring of quality into the mix, though, remember that most quality ratings are not readily available. Most patients have little if any idea if a doctor, hospital, or clinic is high or low quality. They pick providers in the dark, or they choose from quasi-reliable, word-of-mouth references.

Price Not Related to Quality

There is no proven correlation between price and quality. High price does not mean high quality. In fact, the reverse appears to be true. Low price often means an efficient and effective provider and generally high quality. The best choice is cheap and good.

There does appear to be a correlation between volume of procedures and quality. A surgical team that does lots of hips gets good at the procedure. And the better it gets, the more word-of-mouth pulls in clients. Therefore, Serigraph's transparency model displays volumes as well as prices.

Incredibly, the craziness of pricing patterns exists even within the consolidated health care systems. Prices vary widely from one hospital to another within the same organization, from one clinic to a sister clinic. For example, an outpatient heart catheterization at one facility within a large Milwaukee-area health care system runs as little as $4,800, but at another facility within the same system a few miles away, it is priced at as much as $7,700, an internal swing of 60 percent.

What other business sector could get away with a bill several times that of a competitor and then say to the customer: "Don't worry about the bill. It's covered by insurance."

Hospital system managers confess that pricing practices are heavy-handed. Accountants can simply add up their expense increases for the coming year and then figure out how much to bump their rates. Because of government price controls, they can't get necessary increases from the public payers, who account for almost half of the nation's health care spending. So they have to jack up the private side by twice as much. If projected expenses are up 5 percent, for example, the private payers see a 10 percent jump in rates.

This pernicious shift to the private sector will worsen under the new federal law as federal and state governments pick up a bigger share of the population for health care.

There's another area of obfuscation. Health systems will put smaller percentage increases on low-volume procedures and higher percentages on higher-volume procedures. That's where the big money lies. That practice allows the systems to talk about an average increase that does not appear as bad. They use an average of prices, instead of a weighted average.

Hospitals even hire consultants and large staffs to "upcode." That means making sure every line item is billed at the highest possible level. That kind of pressure for maximum revenue from the top of an organization can easily result in pricing irregularities and inconsistencies.

NEED FOR BUNDLED PRICES

Clarity and discipline could be added to the non-system of health care if providers would listen to pleas for bundled billing. Serigraph has long pushed for an all-in-one bill for complex treatments like cancer care.

Our desire for this was triggered when we got one set of bills for $400,000 for a relatively short cancer case, unfortunately terminal. Instead of a single price, it contained hundreds of line items, procedure by procedure, activity by activity, drug by drug. We couldn't understand the bill's countless line items or its subtotals, and, therefore, its total was incomprehensible.

If you pay for procedures, that's what you get: lots of procedures, all piled into out-of-control, inscrutable bills.

The provider's argument was that cancer care is too complex for bundled billing. That doesn't ring true across the board. Some cancers are now treated in a fairly routine way: stage one or two breast cancers, for example, or most prostate cancer treatments. Sadly, there are lots of those cases. Fortunately, medical advances have made many of these cases treatable and no longer fatal.

By the same token, though, those advances are delivered through fairly standard treatments that should lend themselves to standard pricing. Providers could do a bell curve on levels of treatment and price the ones within two standard deviations at a fixed price. We payers could accept cost-plus pricing on the more complex, outlier cases.

As an example, more than 90 percent of new baby deliveries are normal, vaginal births. Why can't there be a set price for the whole episode of care?

If we could get one bundled price, it would allow companies and consumers to get a better handle on what they are facing and get a bead on yearly increases for standard episodes of care. If a natural birth went from $8,000 as a total to $9,000 in the following year, we would identify the 12.5 percent boost, and we could object. We would move business, if necessary.

That doesn't happen now because of the pricing fog.

Here's another example of pricing mismanagement: caesareans earn a higher fee but are actually less work and hassle for doctors. The fix: raise payments for normal deliveries and lower them for C-sections. At the very least they should be priced the same so there is no incentive for an unnecessary C-section.

Until bundled pricing happens, management of large cases will remain a black hole into which the nation's solvency disappears. Serigraph is pushing a fixed price agenda.

Bundled Billing Possible

A number of providers have stepped forward with offers of bundled prices, led by foreign hospitals like Apollo in India. Joint replacements are priced there at about $5,000 total.

We have negotiated bundled prices, also known as global or episodic prices, for simple procedures like colonoscopies, MRIs, and CT scans.

But we have met huge resistance when we ask for bundled prices from the hospital corporations on more complex treatments. Obviously, they like the present system that allows prices increases at will on line items. The pricing opacity suits them.

Despite that inertia, we are making headway. Serigraph cut a deal in early 2010 with BridgeHealth Medical, a new broker offering access to the World-Class Provider Network, a group of leading providers that offers inclusive fixed prices. What a breakthrough! Finally, we have a source of bundled prices from top-notch hospitals, clinics, and doctors.

An example is Aspirus Health of Wausau, Wisconsin, where the quality ratings for heart operations are tops, and the prices are bundled and reasonable.

A sample of the savings from BridgeHealth using all-in, episode pricing is a coronary bypass for $34,000 in the United States, $25,000 in Costa Rica, and $8,500 in India. Compare that to an $80,000 average (after discounts) across the United States!

For another example, take a hip replacement. Through this network a hip replacement in the United States would be $23,000—at least 50 percent below what BridgeHealth cites as the average U.S. price.

To encourage our people to make the longer drives, we offer the following incentives:

- no out-of-pocket costs to the co-worker; company picks up the co-insurance and deductibles;
- all travel costs are covered for patient and companion; and
- coordination of travel and medical issues on both ends.

EXHIBIT 5–1

MEDSAVE REBATES	Cash Rebate to Co-Workers
Diagnostic Test or Outpatient Procedures	
Arm MRI Upper Limb	$250
Back MRI Spine	$250
Breast Biopsy (using special probe)	$250
Breast Mammography (MRI)	$100
Colonoscopy with biopsy	$500
Ear insertion of ventilating tube	$250
Eye Surgery (cataract removal)	$1,000
Gall Bladder Removal (by laparoscope)	$1,000
Groin-Hernia Repair 5 years and older	$325
Hand Surgery (carpal tunnel)	$250
Head CT Scan	$150
Head MRI Brain	$250
Leg MRI Lower Limb	$250
Knee Cartilage Repair (arthroscopy)	$500
Knee Fluid Removal from Joint	$150
Knee Ligament Repair (arthroscopy)	$1,000
Pelvis CT Scan	$150
Stomach CT Scan Abdomen	$150
Stomach Upper Digestive (using endoscopy with biopsy)	$150
Stomach Upper Digestive (using endoscopy)	$150
Tonsils and Adenoids Removal under age 12	$250
Inpatient Procedures	
Back Surgery (laminectomy)	$2,000
Back Surgery (spinal fusion-upper back)	$2,000
Back Surgery (spinal fusion-lower back)	$2,000
Childbirth (normal vaginal delivery)	$500
Childbirth (normal Caesarean section delivery)	$500
Heart (left catheterization)	$2,000
Hip Replacement	$2,000
Hysterectomy, abdominal	$1,000
Knee Replacement	$2,000
Sleep Apnea	$500

Other covered elective procedures are joint replacements, heart valve replacements, spinal fusions, shoulder reconstructions, prostate surgery, and weight-loss surgery. Coverage for plastic surgery is done on a case-by-case basis. In general, reconstructive plastic surgery is covered; vanity procedures are not.

The main attraction of this nationwide network of providers for co-workers, though, may prove to be the high, validated quality ratings in the network (see Chapter 9 for more on quality ratings).

The willingness of some top providers to offer fixed prices raises the question, "Why can't the rest do the same?"

Vendors of other complicated products, like a car or a computer, have set prices. Why not health care?

BridgeHealth brokered about one thousand operations in 2009—not bad for a start-up company.

Serigraph plans to add to its volume. Several employees have already said they would travel in return for free surgery. It's a win-win for company and co-worker. And it will force other providers to respond with equivalent pricing.

Such pure transparency will serve as a cost deflator, a way to reverse some of the out-of-control inflation in the health care sector. It will be a building block for a more dynamic marketplace.

We are not alone in our campaign. Medicare ran pilots in the 1990s on bundled payments for cardiac bypass and cataract removal surgeries. Both experiments provided huge savings, but the more effective pricing model was never adopted.

More than a decade later, more pilots were baked into the national reform.

It's hard to see how anyone could argue about fixed prices, but critics will say that set prices may lead to providers cutting corners at the expense of quality. That's easily solved with transparency and accountability for quality. Do a poor job and you lose repeat business, just like a restaurant.

So we at Serigraph are undeterred. We will move business to Centers of Value that offer us bundled prices. And Anthem is working with us to make that happen.

Indeed, managers of any company have a moral obligation to get to a more manageable cost structure because of the cost-sharing compact with co-workers.

At Serigraph, the 25 percent share sets the levels of premiums for co-workers in the coming year, so we have a mutual interest in managing the costs. We've raised premiums only three times in the last seven years. And we don't want to raise them in 2011.

Large cases are the saddest in personal terms, and also are the cases that wreak the most cost havoc. We had two bad car accidents in 2007 and four major cancer cases. Our costs shot through the roof that year, and we had to raise premiums for 2008.

We carry what's known as stop-loss insurance, but it's costly. We buy coverage for any cases that cost more than $200,000, but the annual premium is $254,000. Our experience with major cases greatly affects the price of the following year's stop-loss premium.

So, the existence of such catastrophic coverage in no way alleviates the need to get large cases under control. The reality, though, is that insurers and third-party administrators do at best a cursory job of managing large cases.

Our MedSave program helps some on big bills, but it doesn't get the job done on really complicated cases. On those, the meter just keeps running and running. One hospital system CEO told me in a moment of candor that even he doesn't understand how those bills accumulate to such ghastly totals.

The MedSave rewards (see Exhibit 5–1) make me feel a little like Robin Hood. We create savings by avoiding providers who gouge and by giving cash back to our co-workers, who make an average of $17 an hour. Nonetheless, we have failed to get catastrophic billing under control. We have yet to tame that particular beast, but we are not giving up.

Bundled prices will be one answer.

CREATING A MARKETPLACE

An added benefit to steering co-workers to Centers of Value that offer rational price structures is the creation of an emerging marketplace.

When one of Serigraph's customers threatens to move its business because of performance or price, we jump. (That doesn't happen very often, but when it does, we move into action.)

Business people know that the best customer is the one you already have. Further, revenue at the margin is all-important to the bottom line. Once over the break-even point, the extra revenues fall quickly and disproportionately to the bottom line. The reverse also happens if business is lost.

That universal truth applies to hospital systems just like every other business. So when employers encourage their employees to act like intelligent consumers, to move their health care business to competitors with better value, then providers, incumbent hospitals, and clinics start to jump, too. Marketplace dynamics take hold.

For several years, our existing MedSave program has offered $250 in cash back to co-workers who took their colonoscopy business to a list of four high-value providers. That cash amount offset the deductible and co-insurance. Now we have gone one step further with the totally free option.

So, what's going to happen to the providers that are charging three, four, or five times as much for their colonoscopies? If they don't change their price, then over time, if enough employees act like consumers, they will be out of business—as they should be.

Their other response would be to lower prices to meet the market. Indeed, that has already happened. Another provider came to us and met the price points of the Milwaukee Endoscopy Center's colonoscopies.

In a related example, Smart Choice MRI offered scans at a fixed price of $600, and we steered our business there.

Subsequently, other providers dropped their prices for Serigraph.

That's how markets are supposed to work. That price competition is what has been missing in health care for decades.

Regina Herzlinger, the Harvard professor who conceptualized the idea of turning an army of consumers loose on health care, maintains that the market only needs to hit a tipping point of about 15 percent of consumers to change the behavior of the providers.

The private sector in Wisconsin has been among the leaders in the country in shifting to high-deductible plans that are offset by personal health accounts. Ironically, in the vanguard are most of the hospital systems and health insurers; they have installed consumer-driven plans for their own employees. No longer are employees insulated from prices because a third-party insurer is paying most of the bills.

One of the major hurdles for moving business is that patients are used to following doctors' orders. That makes some sense on purely medical issues, because the doctor is an expert. But doctors don't usually place business for best price or value. They almost always assign patients to the systems that employ them, regardless of price.

COLLABORATIVE DECISIONS WITH DOCTOR

At Serigraph, we preach that a collaborative relationship between patient and doctor is a better approach to health care decisions than a top-down order from a doctor.

That's the way it's working in society anyway, as consumers gain access to increasing amounts of Web-based information on best practices in health care. There are many sites that help consumers arrive at intelligent medical decisions in concert with their doctors.

On the economic side of medicine, though, the doctors are not experts. When asked, most of them will tell a patient they have no clue about what a procedure costs. No one entirely believes that response, but the inability or unwillingness to answer the question tells us economics are not in the forefront of doctors' minds.

But cost of medicine should be. Economics matter. They matter greatly. Doctors, as well as patients, need to be concerned about the price tag.

In the current state, though, the employee/patient/consumer needs to change the relationship with the doctor, especially on the monetary side of health care. When a doctor automatically refers a patient to a particular test site or hospital, our co-workers at Serigraph have learned to step up and say, "Wait a minute."

"The most important thing is how we [employees] have become aware of challenging things," said Jill Honeck, one of Serigraph's sharpest health care consumers. "We have gotten more bold working with doctors since we went to the new plan."

Our employees check our transparency site for quality, volume, and price, often consulting with our on-site nurse or human resources department for guidance. They then take their business where they get the best value, to a Center of Value.

It is not an easy thing to reverse a doctor's decision on a preferred location, because they are often incentivized through bonuses for keeping patients within their own health care system. The doctors ought to be referring patients to where they get the best value—service, quality, and price—but they don't. They follow the money and refer to where they get their paychecks from or to where it is most convenient for them.

One could make the case that those bonuses ought to be illegal because those payments amount to a restraint of trade.

Consumers have the right to buy their health care where they choose. And the prices for health care have gotten so high and so financially painful that many of them have to move their business to save money.

More Medical Tourism

Though difficult to get a fix on, one estimate said 1.3 million Americans took their health care to foreign countries in 2008 so they could get affordable treatment. In that

NO TRACTION YET FOR MEDICAL TOURISM

Because of our aggressive posture on moving the business, we were approached in 2008 by Anthem to be a test site for medical tourism abroad. Anthem picked the top-flight Apollo Hospital in Bangalore, India, as its initial overseas provider.

It did so because the Apollo Hospital is fully accredited and is staffed by many doctors trained in the West. Apollo's reputation is impeccable.

That program rolled out early in 2009, and we are waiting to see if anyone at Serigraph take us up on our offer of free treatment if they will make the trip to Bangalore. We had no takers through 2011, nor did Anthem. But it's only a matter of time if U.S. prices continue to escalate.

There were many considerations for this overseas expansion of our MedSave program, such as making sure the handoff from U.S. doctors to Indian doctors is rigorous and that the handoff coming back home is equally thorough. Serigraph and Anthem want to make sure the traveling patients are fully accommodated, so they will be met by an English-speaking concierge-type person on their arrival in India. Then an Apollo nurse will be assigned to be the quarterback for the case during the treatment.

We will pay the travel expenses for the patient and a traveling companion, including a stay at a four-star hotel.

The co-worker will see zero cost, and the company will save money.

A typical hip replacement in Milwaukee can cost more than $35,000 at the sticker price. It is delivered for $10,000 in India: about $5,000 for the total surgery bill—surgeon and hospital combined—and $5,000 for the travel package.

Note that Apollo offers a bundled price: there is a single bill.

The traveling patient's co-workers also make out. By holding our total health bill down, we all will enjoy lower premiums the following year.

We subsequently added Costa Rica through BridgeHealth as another foreign option.

If medical tourism succeeds, we will put additional hospitals in other countries on our list of preferred overseas providers. For now, however, it's an experiment without a conclusion.

Already, though, you can see the market start to move. We received a call from a hospital system in Long Beach, California, and its salesperson said it would come close to matching the India price.

---

vein, Serigraph has been one of the pioneers in what some people call "medical tourism." The medical tourism industry is expected to double in just a few years. According to one analysis, the visiting patients are seeking advanced technology and better, faster care, not just lower costs.

We started by selecting high-value providers in southeastern Wisconsin and steering our co-workers to those facilities. One company uses disincentives to do the steerage by doubling the out-of-pocket maximum if an employee goes to any other facility than those on its narrow list of high-value providers. Either carrot or stick can work. We prefer the carrot in the form of cash checks under MedSave.

We have done a lot of digging to find high-value providers across the state. And we now have a recommended list of Centers of Value that is available to all co-workers.

It is understandable that most hospital systems in the United States would resist this new kind of competition. Why would they want to change? They live in an opaque business world where they are unaccountable for costs and prices. If they want to raise prices at the procedure level, the invisible level, they do so with virtual impunity.

With an army of consumer-driven patients coming to the fight, though, they will not be able to operate without penalty. That penalty will be a loss of business.

They have, of course, a perfect remedy: get efficient, revise their business models, get their prices in line, and make the prices and quality ratings transparent.

Hometown providers should have the huge advantage of proximity and convenience, but people will travel to high-value providers in other parts of the region, state, and world if the price discrepancy is too great. If the discrepancy continues to widen, medical tourism will surely grow.

For decades, negotiators for private payers have been jawboning health systems and doctors to get prices down. It hasn't worked. Prices continue to double every eight years. In Wisconsin, 2009 was a relatively good year—prices went up only 7 percent on average. Unfortunately, that's still three times what the inflation index for all goods and services was that year.

In business, if something doesn't work over a period of years, you stop doing it. You take a different tack. That suggests that private payers, those who have the gold, should command the attention of providers on the economic side of medicine by moving the business. If enough companies and consumers move their business, the providers will jump. They will jump high to become competitive Centers of Value.

Name_____

Address_____ Date_____

℞ TAKE-AWAYS ON MAKING A MARKETPLACE

☑ Move your health care to providers with the best value, what Serigraph calls Centers of Value.

☑ Take advantage of price variation across systems and within systems.

☑ Create a marketplace where none now exists.

☑ Pay incentives to employees to get them to select the best medical deals.

☑ Cut deals for bundled prices.

☑ Make care free to employees where deals are really good. Share the savings.

☑ Remember that high price does not mean high quality.

☑ Go abroad or out of your immediate market for elective surgeries if you want real deals.

MD_____

Signature_____

6

THE MISSING LINK: TOP MANAGEMENT AS CHANGE AGENTS

ONE OF MY CEO BUDDIES was fuming about his company's skyrocketing health care costs. He had participated in showdowns in Milwaukee between payer CEOs and CEOs of regional health care systems. They were angry shouting matches.

Still, when I asked my friend how much his company was spending on health care, he couldn't come up with the number, either on a gross basis or per employee. The old management truism says, "You get what you measure," so it was obvious that not much in the way of in-depth management of health care costs was going on in his company, despite his general passion and frustration on the subject.

In general, not many C-level executives are involved in management or leadership on health care issues. That holds true even though health costs are usually the second- or third-largest cost in the company.

Executives usually delegate that responsibility and authority to their human resources departments. HR people are generally good stewards of the existing plan, and they perform well in the system that is framed out for them by providers and insurers. But they are not often change agents in an economic sector badly in need of change. At Serigraph, the two managers of our health care plan in the HR department have become change agents, but they are the exception to the rule.

The health care system isn't a system that works for payers or their employees. It's an economic model that doesn't work. It operates pretty well on the medical side of the equation, but it's mayhem on the business side.

In that dysfunctional environment, routine stewardship is not enough. Because health care delivery, payments, and quality processes are hugely flawed, existing business models need to be completely re-engineered.

The missing link is management—aggressive management—the same kind of management that is applied in many other sides of successful businesses.

Many companies have professionalized their sourcing functions, often taking it to the level of global sourcing. Advanced degrees are offered in the field. So why not professionalize the sourcing of health care? Why tough, professional sourcing is rare in health care is a mystery to me.

Most companies simply run a routine bidding process among insurers every year or two and then take the best deal offered. Even self-insured companies, who are their own risk pool, use a similar routine bidding process to find a network and discounts. This is a shallow exercise that, more often than not, does little to change the practices of providers. Year in, year out, it's business as usual.

Essentially, most private companies trust the big health plans to do their purchasing work for them. That model has not worked well, partly because the health plans are somewhat dependent on the providers for creating their networks. They have a foot in both payer and provider camps. They are middlemen in a busted business model.

I hate the phrase, but what's needed is a paradigm shift. CEOs and CFOs need to grab the non-system by the scruff of the neck and shake it up.

Jim Hagedorn, CEO of Scotts Miracle-Gro, a lawn care products company, did just that. In 2007, he got religion on managing health as a way of attacking health costs. He uses the big-stick *and* big-carrot approach. Hagedorn is famous for firing an employee in the probation period because the recruit refused to stop smoking. At Scotts, you either listen to your health coach or your premiums go up. Their carrot is a huge investment in employee health: a $4 million per year wellness program and a $5 million on-site fitness and medical center manned by two doctors, five nurses, a dietician, a counselor, and two physical therapists.

At KI in Green Bay, Wisconsin, CEO Dick Resch broke the mold when he tied health premium levels to healthiness. There are A, B, C, and D levels of health, determined by annual health-risk assessments. The healthy A players incur very low monthly premiums; the Ds pay the highest rate. KI also promotes a wellness-fitness culture and has an on-site fitness center.

At Serigraph, I am heavily engaged in the promotion of health and the reduction of health costs. Many of our managers are fitness buffs, and we have played them up as positive examples in company publications.

I try to lead by word and by example. At seventy-one, I was on a team of eight older cyclists who competed in the 2008 Race Across America. We did the continent from Oceanside, California, to Annapolis, Maryland, in seven days and twenty-one hours. We raced in rotation day and night and raised $47,000 for the Make-a-Wish Foundation. In 2009, I cross-country skied my fourteenth American Birkebeiner, a hilly, thirty-two-mile course in northeastern Wisconsin.

But this is not about my athletic prowess. I have only modest talent and was slow in both events. This is about C-level leadership.

Search for Best Practices

One of our most reliable management methods at Serigraph is to benchmark aggressively. We seek out best business practices in a broad spectrum of disciplines. We send a team to visit standout companies to learn what they are doing right and bring lessons back to our company for adoption. We have visited dozens of companies that have made innovative changes in health care management and we have adopted their best ideas.

Serigraph is a learning organization. We do not claim to have all the answers; we learn from others, as well as learning internally from each other.

We have not gone as far as KI on A-B-C-D premium levels, but we do charge smokers 10 percent more for their monthly premiums. There has been little adverse reaction from our declining number of smokers, probably because they know full well that their health care will be more expensive than for non-smokers.

Like Scotts and Quad/Graphics, we have an on-site clinic and fitness center. Our clinic has been staffed by a nurse practitioner, a nurse who also acts as a health coach, a dietician, and a chiropractor.

Like Miller Electric in Appleton, Wisconsin, we have established a direct link with a health care system. Aurora Health Care co-manages our diabetic population.

We learned about consumer-driven health plans from Humana.

Like Highsmith in Fort Atkinson, Wisconsin, we have an elaborate point system to reward wellness. The two hundred people at this now-closed distributor of school and library products used the company's fitness program and facilities to help push their health costs 20 percent below the regional average. Taking a page from their book, co-workers at Serigraph can earn up to two "wellness days" off for pursuing healthy lifestyles.

Like S.C. Johnson, we steer our people to centers of excellence that offer the best values for different procedures.

We're totally pragmatic. We find good practices, and we try them out. If they work, they're kept. If not, we toss them.

HEALTH METRICS TRACKED

Any self-respecting management system is grounded in good numbers and analysis. So Serigraph tracks its health and health cost metrics with great rigor. Our consultant compiles an annual dashboard on our key metrics. It is derived from our claims data and sliced and diced with an analytical tool called "Health Plan Intelligence." It is a trove of good information on how we are doing.

Maybe one difference is that the managers at Serigraph take these findings very seriously, and we act on them. As an example, the analysis of 2008 data revealed that 10 percent of our claims were related to unhealthy behaviors. That led us to intensify our attempts to get our co-workers to eat better, to exercise more, and to smoke less.

In the end, lowering health care costs is all about management and a proactive bias versus abstract theorizing. We are not academia or a think tank. We read the theories, but we apply them in the here and now.

CHANGE MANAGEMENT NEVER EASY

It's textbook stuff that the first step in change management is to create a sense of crisis. It serves as a platform for change.

We certainly had no problem outlining the crisis in health care, since health costs were screaming upward at double-digit rates as we entered the decade. Both employee and employer were getting hammered. Our co-workers got the message that we needed an innovative approach to health care.

Our managers, including our HR managers, have learned that starting small with a pilot program is a good way to get the change process started. So, our first year of consumer-driven health care was entirely voluntary. And one option resembled our old standard plan with fairly low deductibles and co-insurance.

The initial round of change worked, so we were emboldened to get even more aggressive in the following years. Along the way, I continually encouraged our health care managers to be bold, to break the mold, to not get stuck in the unacceptable status quo. They are now passionate about reforming the system inside and outside Serigraph.

And we are finding potential savings everywhere in the broken delivery system. We look forward to many years of mining nuggets of savings that will more than offset the general medical inflation.

Politicians talk endlessly about who's covered, who pays, and where to find more money to cover everyone. They miss the main point about controlling inflation because only a few are professional managers. They aim to please, not to solve fundamental problems. They make points, not innovations. Unlike politicians, we have to deal with the real issues: poor health and runaway costs.

The medical side of health care is often brilliant. There is spectacular innovation and intimate care giving. That is not where the problem lies, though there is much room for improvement on quality, including elimination of errors. It is the economic side that's bankrupting the country— all for want of aggressive management, better business models, and realigned incentives for improved economic performance.

CEOs should be embarrassed at how they have allowed health costs to run wild. They would not allow that to happen in any other part of their businesses.

As an example, lean disciplines, backed by quality management tools, have only begun to be applied to health care systems. In other purchases, CEOs insist that their supply chains meet international quality standards like QSO 9000 or TS 16949—the gold standard certifications.

Many will only do business with vendors that have adopted lean disciplines. They often teach these methods to under-performing vendors. But no such demands are made of vendors of health care. Why not?

At Serigraph, we have learned to guide our people to lean vendors. It's part of our MedSave steerage program.

Executives need to understand that the present course of health care inflation is unsustainable. In ten or fifteen years, at present trends, health costs will exceed base pay for employees.

Some engaged CEOs have already bent those trend lines. In short, CEOs can insist that management disciplines be brought to bear on both the payer and provider sides of the equation. Where they have done so, health improves and health care costs come under control.

Name_____

Address_____ Date_____

℞ TAKE-AWAYS ON PROACTIVE MANAGEMENT

- ☑ C-level executives must engage.
- ☑ Turn your health care managers into change agents.
- ☑ Develop new business models; dump those that haven't reduced health care costs.
- ☑ Many best practices are available; find them and apply them.
- ☑ Financially reward healthy behavior.
- ☑ Manage aggressively; do it now.

MD_____

Signature_____

7

Beer, Brats, Butterfat: Health, Lifestyle Can Be Managed

KURT ESCHENFELDER, a former college football player and engineer at Serigraph, stands six feet four inches and tipped the scales at 330 pounds. He looked indestructible. That was until his required health screening showed his blood sugar count at 177, which meant he was pre-diabetic.

Guys like Kurt are commonplace in Wisconsin, where we like our beer, bratwurst, and butterfat (translate: cheese and other dairy products). Typically, in the passive U.S. health care model, Kurt's doctor would have given him a lecture, and Kurt would have been essentially on his own to head off a diabetic condition.

In the proactive model Serigraph has developed, Kurt was surrounded with help. He consulted with Tammy Ertl, our on-site nurse practitioner, Rachel Topercer, a dietician, and Sandy Stockhausen, the diabetes educator from Aurora Health, one of the two big health providers in our area.

Kurt listened, and, unlike most diabetics or near-diabetics, he started a disciplined regimen. He dropped about fifty pounds over six months and lowered his blood sugar to around 100 without medications. Now, Kurt has no other warning signals for diabetes in his physical makeup.

This is the kind of proactive collaboration that the experts propound, yet it happens far too seldom in American medicine. Our dysfunctional non-system pays providers to fix people when they're broken, not to prevent those same health breakdowns. People like Kurt get lost in the big medical complexes.

The avoidance of diabetes in Eschenfelder won't ever show up on the economic ledgers of medicine. His restored health will actually reduce revenues to health providers, with the exception of the small stipend paid to our health coaching team. His health and safety is not a procedure that can be billed, because nothing negative happened. There is now nothing to fix.

Kurt is a healthier, happier guy. His employer will benefit from a more productive worker. His family's budget will be less strapped, and the company's bottom line will be healthier than it would have been had he not made a course correction.

It's a win for everyone but the providers who would have profited had he become sick.

Despite all kinds of talk about prevention and wellness in the medical world, incentives are missing for providers to get serious. Most health systems and insurers make token efforts at wellness education and prevention, such as brochures and passive Web sites. They are largely inert.

In that vacuum, payers like Serigraph have no choice but to take on the challenge themselves, to be very proactive on health management. A principal tool that we deploy is our annual free mini-physicals, known as a Health Risk Assessment The annual process invariably surfaces several time bombs—urgent health conditions that need addressing immediately. (See Exhibits 7-1 and 7-2, my own assessment—note that I have a couple of issues to work on.)

Kurt's situation was not an emergency, but another co-worker faced a more imminent threat. That person recorded a PSA reading of 7.5, a high number that indicated prostate cancer. Fortunately, it is a cancer that is very treatable if caught early. While the Health Risk Assessment yielded unwelcome news, he visited an oncologist that same week. His subsequent treatment was successful. His renewed health was the best outcome. Another positive outcome was the reduced cost to him and the company.

EXHIBIT 7-1

John Torinus

Interra Health: Health Risk Assessment Report
Thank you for participating in this year's Health Risk Assessment
ALL INFORMATION IS COMPLETELY CONFIDENTIAL

Height: 71.00 inches   **Medication:** Chol
Weight: 192 lbs
Self Reported Tobacco Use: No

Summary Table

Category	Your Value	Healthy Range	Risk Level	Points
Nutrition Habits	30	X	Moderate	X
Personal Safety	30	X	Moderate	X
Preventive Exams & Screenings	110	X	High	X
Mens Health*	20	X	Low	X
Skin Health	100	X	High	X
Heart Health*	65	X	High	X
Diabetes Awareness*	5	X	Low	X
Digestive Health*	65	X	High	X
Lung Health	0	X	Low	X
Emotional Health	0	X	Low	X
Blood Pressure (Systolic)	118 mmHg	<130	Low	50
Blood Pressure (Diastolic)	78 mmHg	<90	Low	50
Body Fat	29 %	<22%	High	0
Total Cholesterol	179 mg/dL	<200	Low	100
Cholesterol/HDL	2.89	<3.5	Low	50
HDL	63 mg/dL	>=40	Low	50
Glucose	98 mg/dL	<100	Low	50
LDL	104 mg/dL	<130	Low	50
Triglycerides	65 mg/dL	<150	Low	100
PSA	2.9	X	PSA Negative	0
Body Mass Index	26.6	18.5 - 24.9	Moderate	0
Self Reported Tobacco Use	No	Non-User	Low	350
Total Reward Points				850
Overall Risk Level				Low

*To maintain compliance with the Genetic Information Nondiscriminatory Act (GINA) of 10/7/2009, Interra Health no longer includes family health history questions in our InHealth Risk Assessment. However, family history is still a strong indicator for many diseases, please see your report for more detailed information.

EXHIBIT 7-2

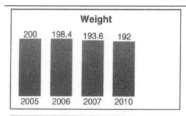

Weight

2005	2006	2007	2010
200	198.4	193.6	192

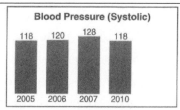

Blood Pressure (Systolic)

2005	2006	2007	2010
118	120	128	118

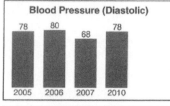

Blood Pressure (Diastolic)

2005	2006	2007	2010
78	80	68	78

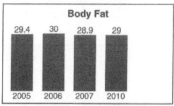

Body Fat

2005	2006	2007	2010
29.4	30	28.9	29

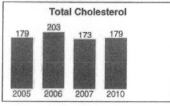

Total Cholesterol

2005	2006	2007	2010
179	203	173	179

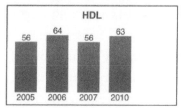

HDL

2005	2006	2007	2010
56	64	56	63

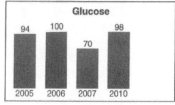

Glucose

2005	2006	2007	2010
94	100	70	98

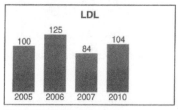

LDL

2005	2006	2007	2010
100	125	84	104

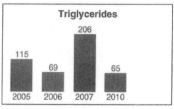

Triglycerides

2005	2006	2007	2010
115	69	206	65

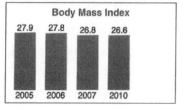

Body Mass Index

2005	2006	2007	2010
27.9	27.8	26.8	26.6

High ■ Mod Low ■ NA ■

97

Early treatment is less expensive than dealing with a full-blown disease. It also saves lives.

We feel so strongly about the necessity of an annual mini-physical that we make them virtually mandatory for employees and their spouses. If you want to be in our health plan, we believe the least you can do is to take the annual physical. You can opt out, but you then pay the full premium for your annual care.

The mini-physicals are not expensive. We contract with our on-site provider, which charges us $45 per person. Using our own nurse practitioner also has the benefit of helping her establish a trusted relationship with our people. Privacy laws in the United States prevent anyone in the company from knowing about those individual conditions, except for the nurse and a benefits specialist. So the nurse is the one who runs the coaching process.

As a bonus, the aggregate health of our group of employees and spouses can be monitored and managed. Company managers can analyze group data without invisible individual data. Again, what you measure is what you get, so Serigraph keeps close track of the biometrics of its population.

For example, doctors now want to see patients below 200 for overall cholesterol, so we track that. We know our average cholesterol number in 2003 was 209. We know that it dropped to 200 by 2006 and has now been reduced even further to 193.

We measured our average systolic blood pressure in 2003 at 128, and we watched it drop by 2006 to 120, the latest target for good health. We saw the same progress on our diastolic reading.

It took Serigraph a couple years to come to the perfectly obvious truth that health costs can't be managed without managing health. Duh!

In 2005, our outside consultant started to analyze each year's claims data to slice and dice our health care performance. Its "dashboard" gives us a benchmark on how well we are managing costs and health. Our most recent analysis, from June 2009, showed that chronic diseases remained a big challenge.

Belatedly, we decided in 2006 to use our professional management skills and tools to tackle those complex health issues. We couldn't wait any longer for our providers to get more proactive.

Our first attempt at proactive health care management targeted diabetes. It is well-known that two-thirds of the diabetics in the United States do not follow their regimens and, therefore, are out of control on three blood tests: A1C, lipids, and cholesterol.

Just as we set a goal of zero defects in manufacturing our products, we set a goal of zero "treatment defects" in the diabetic arena. Obviously, we are not referring to diabetics as defects in the literal sense. We are using that particular Six Sigma term to describe a breakdown in a health management process. In the case of diabetics, that means somebody who is not following his or her regimen.

The first management question was to define the size of the problem. How many diabetics did we have among our employees? We didn't know, and it's fair to assume that most other employers don't know either. The answer came back: forty-nine.

Next question: How many are out of regimen? After another data dig, the answer: sixteen.

Once we had defined the dimension of the problem, the professionals in our on-site clinic were asked to contact all the diabetics and potential diabetics to coach them to follow a regimen similar to what Eschenfelder followed. In some cases, drugs were part of the regimen.

We also dangled an incentive, a $100 bonus to each diabetic for every quarter he or she met standards in three key blood tests. The $400 a year bonus got some attention, but, by 2009, only a disappointing 27 percent had filed for it. The lesson? Money is not as effective an incentive as we had hoped.

Nonetheless, our overall results have been promising. Of our current diabetics (now including spouses), 57 percent are following the protocols for diabetic health.

Similarly, the company started tracking body mass index (BMI) as a metric for obesity. There is a rampant, well-publicized obesity epidemic in the United States, and Wisconsin leads the way. In some years, it is the heaviest of the fifty states per capita (other years, it is second, behind Texas). Not exactly a trophy to covet.

Serigraph employees are not exempt from those trends. Unfortunately, unlike diabetes and blood pressure, where we had some success, we did not move the needle on BMI from 2003 to 2008. We were stuck at a BMI of 30. A good number would be less than 25.

As with any quality system, we went back to the drawing board to try to figure out the root cause of our inability to get the attention of our co-workers on this chronic disease.

Behavior change of food and beverage consumption is very difficult for almost everybody. So we asked focus groups of employees what they thought would work.

Again, it is part of the philosophy of Serigraph and lean enterprises to engage every single employee in solving problems. The result in 2009 was a retooled weight loss and exercise program called "Get LEAN!" (Lose weight, Exercise, Attitude, Nutrition) and included a "Move Around the World Fitness Challenge." The early returns on this program were very positive, with ninety employees initially enrolling in the programs.

In the first twelve weeks of the 2010 program, fifty-four determined co-workers dropped 517 pounds. Partly because people sign up in teams, developing some peer pressure in the process, almost all those enrolled have accomplished reductions, including some surprisingly large losses.

That's major progress, especially since our data shows that an obese co-worker costs our health plan $24,227 per year—more than three times our average co-worker.

Seminars and presentations abound in the health care industry about why hyper-inflation in health care exists and why it is inexorable. At every one of those seminars,

THE COMPANY THAT SOLVED HEALTH CARE

EXHIBIT 7-3

Let Wellness Work for You!
Earn additional paid-time off by participating in Serigraph's wellness program!

Did you know that you can earn up to 2 days of paid-time off by participating in Serigraph's wellness program?

Program Incentives
In order to be eligible for program incentives, participants must complete the *InHealth BioScreen*™ and earn at least 1200 points. All participants must be active employees at the time of disbursement in order to receive their reward.

If it is unreasonably difficult or medically inadvisable for you to attempt to achieve the points for a reward under this program, *Interra Health*™ will work with you to develop an alternative way to earn points to qualify for a reward.

Reward Levels	Level 1	Level 2	Level 3	Level 4
Reward	4 Hours PTO	8 Hours PTO	12 Hours PTO	16 Hours PTO
Points Needed	1200	1400	1600	1800

Your InHealth BioScreen™ Score
Based on your InHealth BioScreen™ results you will be given:
- A risk rating (High, Moderate, or Low) for each test
- An overall health risk rating
- Points for each screening category (see table below)

InHealth™ BioScreen	Low Risk Values	Low Risk Points	Moderate Risk Values	Moderate Risk Points	High Risk Values	High Risk Points
Tobacco Use	Non-User	350	n/a	n/a	User	0
Blood Pressure	≤ 129/89	100	≤ 159/99	50	≥160/100	0
Total Cholesterol	≤ 199	100	≤ 239	50	≥ 240	0
HDL	≥ 40	50	35 – 39	25	≤ 34	0
LDL	≤ 129	50	≤ 159	25	≥ 160	0
HDL Ratio	≤ 3.54	50	3.55 – 4.99	25	≥ 5.00	0
Triglycerides	≤ 149	100	≤ 199	50	≥ 200	0
Glucose	30 – 99	50	100 – 126	25	≥ 127	0
Female Body Fat	F <28%	100	F 28-32.9%	50	F ≥ 33%	0
Male Body Fat	M < 22%	100	M 22 -27.9%	50	M ≥ 28%	0
BMI	< 25	50	25 -29.9	25	≥ 30	0
Total Possible Points = 1000						

Proprietary Information. Copyright © 2010 *Interra Health*™. All Rights Reserved.

102

EXHIBIT 7-3 (continued)

In addition to earning wellness points from your *InHealth BioScreen™*, you can earn wellness points by participating in approved wellness programs and activities throughout the year. Participants have between January 1ˢᵗ, 2010 and December 31, 2010 to earn wellness points for the 2010 wellness program.

2010 Approved Wellness Programs & Activities	Points Earned
InHealth Coaching™	
Lifestyle Management Education Programs (complete program)	200/program
Coaching Sessions	25/session
Dietitian (maximum 6/yr)	
Dietitian Visits (excludes CTRL + ALT + DEL requirements)	25/session
Personal Training	
Exercise Orientation (1 maximum)	100
Personal Training (maximum 6 per year)	25/session
Preventative Exams & Screenings	
InHealth BioScreen™	1000 (max)
InHealth Risk Assessment™ (must be completed by 3/20/10)	50
Fecal Occult Blood Test (Colon Cancer Screen) – M/F 50+	100
Colonoscopy – M/F 50+	100
Mammogram – F 40+	100
Pap Smear/Clinical Breast Exam – F	100
PSA Test – M 50+	100
Digital Rectal Exam – M 50+	100
Annual Physical/Check-up – M/F	200
Annual Vision Exam – M/F	50
Dental Checkup (2X year) – M/F	50/per check up
Annual Flu-Shot – M/F	50
Additional Activities	
Walks/Runs/Bike Rides	25
CTRL + ALT + DEL Weight Management Program (12 week program)	100/program
Be Active Fitness Challenge	Based on Level Reached
Lunch & Learns/Wellness Seminars	25/seminar
Approved Weight Management Program (e.g. Weight Watchers 6 month minimum)	100
Approved Smoking Cessation Program (individual or group)	350
Blood Donation (maximum 2/year)	25/donation
Onsite Blood Pressure Screening (maximum of 4/year)	15/screening
CPR/AED Certification	100
Community Volunteering (maximum 4/year)	25/event
Monthly Newsletter Quiz	10
Other (must be approved by Health Coach, e.g., Yoga, Tai Chi, etc.)	TBD

Submitting Activity Verification for Wellness Points

To earn wellness points for wellness program participation, *Interra Health™* requires participants to submit a verification form for the activities they have completed. Verification forms can be obtained through Human Resources or the Serigraph Health Center located in Plant 1.

- Wellness points for participation in programs conducted by *Interra Health™* are automatically awarded; no additional documentation is required (e.g. *InHealth Coaching™* sessions).
- Documentation must be submitted for any other approved program or activity. Interra Health™ will verify the authenticity of all documentation prior to awarding wellness points.
- Accepted forms of documentation include, but are not limited to: registration forms, attendance forms, doctor/clinic notes, Explanation of Benefit (EOB) forms, and medical bills.

All documentation must be received by Interra Health™ no later than December 31, 2010 in order to receive points for the 2010 wellness program. Late documentation will not be accepted.

the 80/20 rule is rolled out—20 percent of the people in a population cause 80 percent of health costs. They are the people with chronic disease conditions. Sometimes the ratio estimate is 90/10.

Whatever the percentage, no manager can claim to be doing a good job with health costs if he or she isn't tackling health issues head on. Any organization without an aggressive program to keep people well and out of the hospital, especially those with chronic diseases, is hurting itself. You don't need a treatise on epidemiology or macroeconomics to figure out that one.

Our own data for 2008 showed that 14 percent of Serigraph members were treated for one of the six prevalent chronic diseases (coronary disease, obesity, high blood pressure, depression, asthma, or diabetes). That 14 percent was responsible for 55 percent of our health costs. The case is closed on the need to address those six killers!

Further, their claims averaged $10,078 per person, or seven times that of members without chronic diseases in our health plan.

What more needs to be said about the need to manage chronic diseases as part of a health-cost initiative?

Admittedly, the benefits of behavior change to remedy or mitigate conditions of chronic disease are longer term than the attention span of most managers. In most companies, they are invisible. They result in problems not happening. They are cost avoidance. The savings are difficult to measure.

Nonetheless, a number of longitudinal studies have shown that the payoffs are $3–$4 of savings for every dollar spent on prevention and wellness. That's big enough leverage to not quibble with the numbers. It's a big enough payoff, not only in terms of dollars but in terms of human happiness, to move to action, to not suffer paralysis by analysis.

So what is Serigraph doing for prevention? For openers, we make all prevention tests free. That means mammograms and Pap tests for women and PSA tests for men are part of the free annual assessments. We now make colonoscopies free if purchased at a Center of Value. In addition, up to $500 per person in prevention is free to the co-worker.

Because it just makes sense to be serious about the health of your employees, we have adopted many best practices for our wellness and prevention program. The components include:

- an elaborate point system (see Exhibit 7–3) for wellness rewards;
- no paid sick days are allowed because they can be abused, but wellness days offset that need;
- a 10 percent higher premium for smokers;
- coaching for co-workers who have health issues;
- a free, on-site dietician, nurse practitioner, and chiropractor, who doubles as our ergonomics expert;
- a free primary care doctor whose mission includes prevention, wellness, and chronic disease management;

- formal programs for chronic diseases;
- promotion of a fitness culture;
- tracking health metrics of our co-workers;
- walking paths around our campus;
- an on-site fitness center;
- sponsorship and participation in walking, running, and biking events.

Early on, we asked our people what incentives would help the most with behavior change. The answer was a resounding "Time off!" Gift certificates didn't cut it. Time off did. That probably is a reflection of the fact that Americans work more hours than workers in almost any other country.

So we came up with "wellness days"—days of vacation earned by good results in the Health Risk Assessment or activities that lead to better metrics. Top performers can earn four half days of added vacation, or two extra days.

At the beginning of the program, we used an honor system for reporting behaviors like wearing seat belts, smoking, and drinking amounts.

We have since gravitated to mostly hard metrics from the annual health risk assessment. The mini-physical captures nicotine use, as well as cholesterol, blood pressure, and BMI.

The 2010 version awards two wellness days off at 1,800 points. Up to a thousand points can be earned by co-workers who take part in the full battery of prevention exams and screenings. Education programs also earn points.

The program is not all that expensive. It cost the company about $7,500 for time off in 2009. If we avoid one episode of care for a chronic disease, we save money.

Beyond the direct benefits, the wellness program serves to inculcate a health ethic across the company. The co-workers have tangible evidence (days off) that we want them to lead healthful lives. Such lives will be less expensive as well, for them and for the company.

Unfortunately, less than one quarter of the co-workers at Serigraph apply for the extra time off. And some of those would lead healthful lives regardless of the rewards. We are working toward a higher percentage. And we are sticking with the program, despite its low numbers, because we believe it helps to establish our wellness/fitness culture.

Many of the managers of the company try to lead the way and set an example as fitness buffs. The joke in the company is that you have to do a marathon of some sort in order to get promoted.

The fitness culture we work to instill is a far cry from the booze culture that pervaded the old Serigraph. Prior to my purchase of the company in 1987, most of the company legends had to do with alcohol. It was a carryover from the three-martini lunch that was part of corporate life when I broke into the business world in the 1960s.

While I am far from a teetotaler (red wine is medicinal, after all), one of my first official acts was to ban drinking at lunch. That drastically cut the revenues at the Coachman House, the local watering hole for a good number of the free spirits at the company.

Instead, we brag up fitness successes, like the ten Serigraphers who cross-country ski the American Birkebeiner, a fifty-kilometer marathon that attracts eight thousand skiers to Wisconsin.

We still have a lot of work ahead of us on wellness and prevention. As we learn more about disease management, we will keep adding other diseases to our active management list, like asthma and high blood pressure.

We have studied the prevention/wellness programs of other companies, like Pitney Bowes and Scott Gro, which won't hire smokers. Neither will the Cleveland Clinic.

Our smoker percentage dropped from 31 percent in 2008 to 23 percent in 2009. We started high, but are now near the U.S. average.

Highsmith, the now-closed catalog company, used an intense wellness/fitness program as its primary tool and kept its costs at about $1,000 per employee below its peer group.

Highsmith's pioneering helped Serigraph's leaders to become believers that health can be aggressively managed in a corporate setting and that it is essential to controlling costs in the long and short run. Highsmith believed, as we do, that collateral benefits are higher energy and productivity on the job, fewer absences, better attitudes, and improved mental health. These positive results are hard to quantify in dollars, but the payoffs are obvious.

As with tuition reimbursement, employees perceive the company as committed to them when investments are made in their personal health. A full health plan can be a morale booster.

Besides, it's just the right thing to do.

Name_____

Address_____ Date_____

℞ TAKE-AWAYS ON LIFESTYLE CHANGE, CHRONIC DISEASE MANAGEMENT

☑ Annual Health Risk Assessments are inexpensive yet highly effective. Make them virtually mandatory.

☑ The overall health of a company's population can be sharply improved.

☑ Metrics are critical to health management, for each individual and for the group as a whole.

☑ Chronic diseases, the driver of 80 percent of health costs, must be managed.

☑ Obesity should be managed just like other chronic conditions.

☑ Providing incentives to stay healthy can help.

MD_____

Signature_____

Primacy of
Primary Care
Delivers Big Savings

D R. RAYMOND ZASTROW runs an innovative
health clinic that encourages its forty doctors to
spend as much time with patients as necessary.
They don't do the eight-minute, in-and-out office visits
that primary care doctors in big health systems—better
described as non-systems—are incentivized to do.

His doctors deliver medicine the old-fashioned way. They listen. They put the patient at the center. Visits are often thirty to forty-five minutes.

Zastrow heads QuadMed, a subsidiary of one of the most innovative companies in America, Quad/Graphics, a leading global printer of magazines. Harry Quadracci, its founder, and Dr. Len Quadracci, his Johns Hopkins-educated brother, came to the conclusion twenty years ago that they needed to take control of the front end of the medical-delivery system. With six thousand employees in the Milwaukee area, they had the critical mass to set up their own primary care clinic.

They now operate eight clinics, five for their own employees in three states, two for Briggs & Stratton, and one for MillerCoors. Several more clinics for other corporations are in the works.

The Quad model has been instructive to Serigraph, which has followed its lead. It should be instructive to the national challenge on how to deliver quality health care at a reasonable cost. Its model is paying off in patient satisfaction, improved health, and cost control.

QuadMed has performed consistently below benchmarks for costs by a significant percentage. On an adjusted basis for demographics and plan design, the consulting firm Mercer put Quad at 18 percent below its Midwestern peers in 1998. By 2006, Quad enjoyed a cumulative reduction of 32 percent below peers (see Exhibit 8-1).

Those are major savings. They are valid. They are reproducible elsewhere.

EXHIBIT 8-1: RESULTS FROM QUADMED

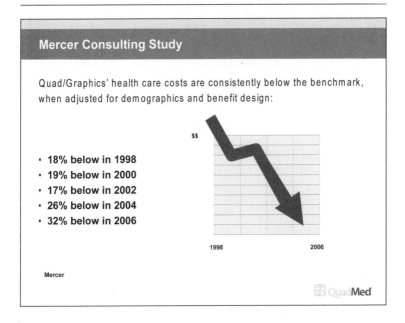

Mercer Consulting Study

Quad/Graphics' health care costs are consistently below the benchmark, when adjusted for demographics and benefit design:

- **18% below in 1998**
- **19% below in 2000**
- **17% below in 2002**
- **26% below in 2004**
- **32% below in 2006**

$$

1998   2006

Mercer

QuadMed

Serigraph's 2008 per-life medical cost was $3,640, a number achieved with aggressive management, a consumer-driven plan, and lots of intelligent consumerism from its co-workers.

In the same year, Quad, without the benefit of a consumer-driven plan, did better at $3,135 per life. Public payers in the state, by comparison, are two or three times those numbers, because they are stuck in traditional, under-managed plans that lack sufficient incentives and use excessive amounts of specialty care.

Cost savings are not the only reason that companies are moving toward on-site medical clinics that they own or control. They do it so they can turn the upside-down delivery of health care right-side up.

They do it so they can regain command of the delivery of health care. If you manage the front end of the process, you have a fighting chance to put a tourniquet on the hyper-inflation inflicted by the industry on the nation. And you can control quality more effectively.

Over the past couple of decades, the big health care companies have ruled the front end of medicine by buying up clinics and doctors in just about every market. They have amassed power on the supply side, partly in response to insurance pools amassing the power of big numbers of members on the demand side.

The providers profess that their acquisitions of clinics are done to accomplish integrated care, but they do it mainly for business reasons. Their business model of vertical integration allows them to control the entrance to their systems. The clinics are instructed to ship their sickest patients to their secondary-care clinics and tertiary-care hospitals. The system-employed doctors seldom refer outside their own corporations.

They have been so acquisitive that there are few independent doctors left in most urban markets.

What we have, then, is a go-nowhere stalemate between powerful provider organizations and powerful insurance companies where prices keep rising relentlessly. Accordingly, the right response for payers is to hire their own gatekeepers to regain the steerage into or out of the expensive systems.

Once providers successfully consolidate into monopolies, duopolies, or triopolies, antitrust laws be damned, they call the shots. Invariably, that means a huge tilt toward treatment by specialists instead of by nurses, nurse practitioners, physician assistants, and primary care doctors.

As Dr. Zastrow puts it, the pyramid is upside down. In the way the big systems do business today, the specialists deliver most of the care, at least in dollar terms.

Broken U.S. System   Reformed Quad System

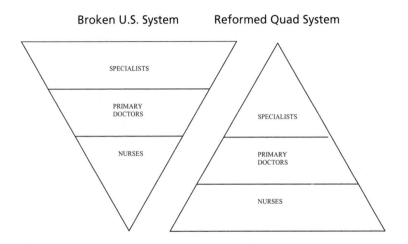

Why would that be?

As always, when things are running amok, follow the money. The big hospital systems can bill substantially more for specialty work than for primary care, so they do. They then tilt heavily to specialty care to pad the bottom line.

And medical students aren't dense. They employ the same philosophy Willie Sutton did in the 1920s and '30s. Asked why he robbed banks, he said, "That's where the money is." Only a small minority of medical students are now opting for primary care. They graduate with big student loans and then go where the money is—specialty care.

That's the medical economic world created by pricing mismanagement, led by the federal government. Nonetheless, private companies, which can't endlessly tap taxpayer resources, have to figure out a better business model. That's what Quad did two decades ago.

It put primary care back at the forefront, which allows the company to deliver quality, very personal care the old-fashioned way—with the patient at the center of the process.

It's catching on. Nearby, Kohl's Department Store has installed an on-site clinic that serves its 3,500 employees at its headquarters. The clinic operates with one general practitioner, several nurses, a physical therapist, a health educator, and a separate pharmacy. Kohl's started with a contract with Walgreen's, which has moved into the market for on-site delivery of medicine.

The world's largest private software company, SAS Institute, employs four doctors and a dozen nurses on its three-hundred-acre campus in Cary, North Carolina. Its primary care is free, and the company estimates that this model saves $5 million per year in medical costs.

Through 2009, Serigraph didn't have enough critical mass to justify a doctor on-site. But we did establish an on-site clinic in 2004 headed by a nurse practitioner and a chiropractor. Later we added a nurse-coach and a dietician.

The move to an on-site clinic has worked well for us in many dimensions: disease management, prevention, intimacy of care, cost reduction, and steerage toward value.

The Quad model isn't just about convenient primary care. Its reforms are really a bottom-up reform of health care. In contrast, the political dialogue in Washington, D.C., has been mostly about access, who pays, coverage limits, and which entities have the power in the industry. The result is a law that is not about what works in terms of delivery.

QuadMed is about what works. Here are some of its important building blocks:

■ **Doctors on Salary**
   Quad doctors are paid mostly by base salary, with some small incentives for quality and productivity. That stands in stark contrast to most systems which pay doctors by procedures. If you were paid by procedure, what would you do? You would do lots of procedures; you would see forty or more patients a day, just like they do in the big systems. (Manufacturers got rid of piece-rate pay geared to units of output a generation ago, because we got lots of production but lousy quality.) Quad doctors attain the job satisfaction that motivated them to go to medical school in the first place. Their turnover is very low. Cleveland Clinic, another innovator, also uses a base pay model to eliminate the incentive to run up the number of procedures.

- **All Electronic Records**

  Each patient/employee using QuadMed has an electronic medical record, but it isn't just about going paperless. The electronic system is used proactively to help the Quad doctors deliver better care. It tells a doctor, for instance, if diabetic patients are in or out of control. The medical record system looks at patients as a group, or it can drill down on an individual patient. The system prompts the doctor and the patient when a foot, eye, or blood test is overdue. With chronic diseases causing 80 percent or more of health costs, this proactive management yields huge dividends in avoided illnesses and hospital admissions.

- **Prevention Prominent**

  Education and incentives to stay out of hospitals figure prominently in the Quad approach. Diabetics, for instance, receive free supplies and medicines to help them stay in control of their blood chemistries. Doctors receive regular electronic report cards on their patients' compliance or non-compliance with evidence-based protocols for chronic disease management. This spurs them to get up to par.

- **Inexpensive Office Visits**

  Quad employees pay only $6 for an office visit. Catching conditions early and heading them off is a key piece of strategy. Quad uses a network of secondary- and tertiary-care providers in its regions, but the aim is to keep its people from needing expensive specialty care. Quad's employees spend 21 percent less time in hospitals than the national average.

■ **Medical Home**

At the heart of the Quad delivery model is integrated care. Its personnel and systems create what has become known as a medical home, a place all records on an employee are kept in a confidential electronic file, and where doctors and nurses rigorously coordinate tests, imaging, regimens, prescriptions, and treatments. This seamless management eliminates the problem of disconnected treatments that plague big hospital systems. If employers don't have enough critical mass to create on-site medical homes, they should insist that their providers do so. Quad's on-site pharmacy pushes generic drugs and the elimination of medication errors. An eye care shop is also on-site. One of its clinics employs three dentists, recognizing that dental hygiene is critical for overall health.

■ **Fitness Centers, Employee Assistance Program On-Site**

Quad facilities include fitness centers to encourage wellness. Physical therapy is available in their clinics. The Employee Assistance Program for help with personal problems is also on-site. That can involve help on anything from depression to addictions to budget problems.

QuadMed has achieved its sterling cost-effectiveness without converting to a consumer-driven health plan, making its results all the more remarkable.

A 2008 Watson Wyatt study showed that 51 percent of U.S. payers had adopted consumer-driven plans. That quiet revolution has started to make health care look more like a marketplace, but as more Americans are converted to public payer plans under ObamaCare, the battle will be at full roar to determine if consumerism and market dynamics can survive.

As for Quad, it could save more money if it converted from its low-deductible approach to a consumer-oriented mentality. The company's paternal philosophy, however, may prevent the use of high deductibles and offsetting health accounts.

There are different ways to get to effective management of health care and health costs, and that is the beauty of a private marketplace and the innovation it brings. Quad's is one of the best models. Smaller firms can employ variations of the Quad model (see Chapter 13).

Note that QuadMed's reported costs include all facets of care. So the validity of its financial savings is unassailable. If anything, their success is understated.

At Serigraph, our nurses do several more critical functions. They help steer employees to the best providers for quality, service, and price—to Centers of Value. Our on-site professionals personally conduct the required annual mini-physicals, including blood draws. They coach people with chronic conditions, such as asthma, obesity, high-blood pressure, and, often, depression.

Our chiropractor fixes aches and pains but also heads to the factory floor or offices to address ergonomic issues, such as carpal tunnel from poorly designed repetitive motions. The company has eliminated most harmful movements through his direct intervention. Our safety metrics are the best in our sixty-year history.

In early 2010, we made an acupuncturist available to co-workers for a small charge.

All the on-site primary care at Serigraph is free to the co-worker. The company takes the business risk that good care at the primary level will more than pay for our clinic costs through savings elsewhere and down the road.

Often, for instance, a visit to our nurses eliminates an office visit with a doctor.

If our prevention program works, the avoidance of just one day in a hospital saves five grand or more. Our internal analysis confirms that the savings outweigh the costs of the free, up-front primary care. When the pyramid is right-side up, everyone wins.

There is always an issue of trust with on-site medical delivery. Over time, though, employees come to know that clinic records really are confidential, that they won't be used in employment decisions like pay or promotion. They come to trust the on-site professionals. They come to know that the company will not invade their medical privacy. They come to believe that the company cares deeply about their health and their pocketbooks concerning health care.

Free primary care demonstrates concern for employees in a very personal, fundamental way.

One of the great attractions of the on-site facilities is convenience. It's right there at the workplace. That alone, coupled with free care or very low out-of-pocket expense, encourages more people to use health care when they need it.

Toward Direct Care

It is encouraging that the emphasis on primary care is expanding elsewhere at the ground level in the private sector. New direct-care companies are getting into the game. New competitors, like MD^2, MDVIP, and ModernMed, are taking on the sprawling health systems and are delivering what is called direct care, retainer care, concierge care, or preventive care. For an annual fee of about $600 to $1,800 and up, doctors in these franchises deliver personal care to a small group of patients.

They serve three hundred to five hundred patients instead of the patient load of twenty-five hundred or more for most big systems. They integrate care. They take calls 24/7. They offer next-day appointments. They oversee the care their patients get from specialists and hospitals. They even make house calls.

The very existence of the concierge doctor sector, as well as its growth, speaks to the weaknesses of the massive health care organizations. Doctors on retainer had grown to more than five thousand by 2010.

Jami Doucette, the young doctor who formed ModernMed to emphasize preventive care, maintains that early returns from his kind of delivery model can cut hospitalizations by 65 percent to 80 percent. That goes right to the heart of managing the most expensive, most out-of-control part of U.S. medicine.

The young Milwaukee native holds a medical degree and MBA from Tufts. His delivery model includes, among other elements, an annual executive-level physical for everyone under its care, not just executives. The average Joe gets VIP treatment. Doesn't that make sense?

The mini-physicals delivered at Serigraph have helped a lot, but full physicals annually make even more sense.

It makes so much sense that Serigraph rolled out a free program in late 2009 with ModernMed and, in particular, Dr. Mark Niedfeldt.

Dr. Niedfeldt hooked up with ModernMed because he became very dissatisfied with the way medicine was being delivered in the big system that employed him. "Primary care had become a stepchild," he said. "Just feed the system, order tests, and refer to specialists." That's not the way he wanted to practice.

Most of ModernMed's patients come in as individual customers looking for better care. Other concierge or direct-care doctors market the same way. In a major departure, Serigraph became ModernMed's first corporate customer. Dr. Niedfeldt stood up in front of all our employees and explained over several meetings that he is all about intimate primary care.

"Will you really make house calls?" one co-worker asked. He answered that if the medical situation calls for it, then "yes."

His background is primary care and sports medicine. He counts Milwaukee Bucks basketball players, Milwaukee Wave soccer players, and Milwaukee Ballet dancers among his patients. He must have impressed our employees. We expected maybe 50 people out of the 1,230 lives on our plan to sign up for the pilot program, but 130 signed on right out of the chute. Some of his hours will be at Serigraph, some at his office twenty minutes away. For openers, he works at the company clinic from 8:30 A.M. to 11:30 A.M. every Tuesday. He will expand those hours as demand grows.

Dr. Niedfeldt works closely with our existing on-site medical staff to systematically improve the health of the Serigraph community. He is helping us individually and collectively to make progress on overall heath metrics.

Serigraph had been trying to figure out a way to employ a doctor directly for years, but never could justify the cost of a full-time physician. The ModernMed franchise model fits what we need. We can contract for as many of his patient slots as we need. We pay a flat annual fee for each family member.

Mid-size employers are adding ModernMed doctors across the country.

We are elated to offer this intimate service, and we're confident that Doucette and Niedfeldt are on the right track. They will take medicine back to a patient-centric model. Their revolutionary initiative will deliver care that is better and costs far less than the current mainstream system.

FINDING GOOD DEALS

Another huge benefit from having primary doctors dedicated to their patients is their ability and willingness to guide them to the best Centers of Value for other treatments. Doctors know who the good doctors are. They know or can learn where good deals for health care are.

As an example, Dr. Niedfeldt refers Serigraph people to a firm called Body Renovation for physical therapy. It charges $90 per hour, about the Medicaid reimbursement, while competing shops charge retail rates of $400 to $500 per hour.

Serigraph and its on-site staff now affect the entry to the complex and expensive medical providers. We become the gatekeepers.

Serigraph co-workers also can use our chiropractor for physical therapy. He does a fine job for no extra charge. And it's free to co-workers.

Essentially, they at ModernMed and we at Serigraph are reinventing the relationship between patient and physician and between payer and provider. It's a new high-touch model for care and the cost of care.

It doesn't take an act of faith for a company to go this route. The audited numbers at QuadMed, gathered over two decades, prove beyond any reasonable doubt that primary care should be the pivotal platform for value-based medicine. Effective primary care saves huge sums of money.

As further evidence on that proposition, Dr. Jeff Thompson, CEO of Gundersen Lutheran Health Care in La Crosse, Wisconsin, has taken intense primary care into a Medicare population. He points to the reality that 5 percent of Americans, usually older people, account for 50 percent of the nation's health bill. Cutting it even finer, 1 percent of Americans account for 25 percent of the total health costs in the United States. Thompson's response was to assign a team headed by a physician's assistant to a group of seniors. Their previously piece-meal care became integrated, and total costs plummeted.

Unfortunately, his experiment was killing his finances. He wasn't getting reimbursed for the team's exemplary work. He was keeping the seniors more healthy and out of the hospital, spelling a revenue reduction. So he couldn't afford to push past his pilot project. His was another effective innovation that ended up on the rocks of a busted economic model for health care.

Again, changing the Medicare pricing policy to reward primary care would solve that nonsensical dynamic. All Medicare patients should have a medical home, and the savings would flow.

A prediction: the big health organizations, with their bloated cost structures and insensitive service, will have to respond with some form of medical home, including a fixed price for primary care. They will move to a fundamentally more engaged relationship between patients and frontline doctors.

Name_____

Address_____ Date_____

℞ TAKE-AWAYS ON PRIMARY CARE EMPHASIS

- ☑ Free or low-priced clinics can markedly improve the delivery of health care.

- ☑ Primary care must be restored to its rightful place as the foremost provider in any delivery system.

- ☑ Medical homes must be established to provide seamless care.

- ☑ Overall health costs drop dramatically when employers emphasize primary care, especially on-site care.

- ☑ Primary care that is owned by payers gives them control of the pivotal front end of the medical world, helping them to resist automatic steerage to high-priced specialists and hospitals.

- ☑ Care in on-site clinics can be far more intimate and organized than big hospital systems.

- ☑ New competitors allow payers to contract on a flexible basis for any primary care needed by their employees.

MD_____

Signature_____

9

QUALITY RATINGS ELUSIVE, BUT ESSENTIAL

UNLIKE MOST of his industry, Dr. Fernando Riveron competes on quality. The numbers for his twelve-doctor team for cardiac care in Wausau, Wisconsin, speak for themselves.

His team scored a perfect 100 on a quality scale for three different heart procedures. The track record of his cardiac unit at Aspirus Health, part of a health system in central Wisconsin, allows it to advertise as "the best heart care for

60,000 miles." That's the length of the arteries, veins, and capillaries in the human circulatory system. How refreshing: ads based on quality statistics.

Most heart centers use an external heart-lung machine four out of five times for bypass surgery, a process that causes all kinds of nasty complications. Dr. Riveron and his unit at Aspirus Health pioneered bypass operations "off pump," which they employ 94 percent of the time. They graft their bypass repairs directly on the beating heart. Instead of lifting a patient's heart out of their chest and temporarily replacing it with a mechanical contraption, the heart continues to pump during the operation. Riveron picked up that best practice from innovative surgeons in Brazil.

Though questioned for effectiveness in one study, that kind of breakthrough, coupled with Six Sigma-level analysis of all defects in the delivery of its cardiac treatments, has yielded some impressive results compared to national averages:

- a lower mortality rate by 40 percent;
- a 5.5 day hospital stay versus 7.9 nationally;
- half as many pneumonia cases;
- zero incidents of sterna infection from 2004 to 2007; and
- 8.8 percent of heart patients readmitted within thirty days versus 9.4 percent nationally.

When one of Aspirus' metrics goes in the wrong direction, immediate analysis and corrective actions are undertaken.

Dr. Riveron's rankings come from a thirty-year-old quality database maintained by the Society of Thoracic Surgeons (STS). Of the one thousand major heart centers in the country, about 75 percent send in their data voluntarily, so these are solid numbers.

Curiously, that data and other internal quality measures are seldom released by most medical providers. Why not? What are they afraid of showing?

Clearly, the fear of not looking good against competitors and the possibility of giving ammunition to trial lawyers in malpractice cases override the needs, even rights, of customers to know the facts about quality outcomes.

Does the doctor or hospital do a good job or a bad job on categories of procedures? Those of us who pay the bills should collectively demand transparency of quality data. That happens in most parts of the business world. Why not in health care?

The Cleveland Clinic, one of the most innovative health care systems, deploys advanced quality methods, and it makes its outcome data available to inquiring patients and payers. Aspirus and Cleveland prove transparency is possible.

STEER TOWARD QUALITY

Not surprisingly, then, Serigraph is steering its co-workers and their families to Aspirus for heart operations.

Another approach for buyers of health care would be quality audits, which are routine in manufacturing. Almost every month, a major customer descends on Serigraph to perform a quality audit. The auditors dig deep into our processes to see if we are good enough to be their supplier. They look at everything from plant cleanliness to scrap rates and from corrective action protocols to training regimens.

You pass the audit, you get the business. You fail, you don't.

Often, vendors are given a list of non-conformances to fix. The end result of repeated audits and an unrelenting demand for accountability and corrective actions is much improved vendor performance.

Some interest by payers has developed in quality audits of health care vendors. But CEOs have been mostly silent. They have not yet found the collective voice to make it happen. You would think they would order their buying agents, the health insurers, to demand quality information.

Common sense tells us to ferret out which are the best and worst providers. To passively give our health care dollars to providers with poor outcomes amounts to dereliction of our duty as leaders of companies.

"The health care delivery system is fundamentally flawed because of the uncoupling of costs and outcomes," said Dr. Riveron.

There is a bell-shaped curve of quality among doctors, doctor-nurse teams, clinics, and hospitals, just as there is in any field of human activity. How then can we justify a blind selection process that sends our people to the care-givers on the poor performance end of the spectrum?

Serigraph uses a variety of sources to try to judge quality.

First, our home-grown transparency system shows volumes of procedures. We want to know whether a surgery team, for example, performs six hundred hip replacements a year or six. Evidence supports a correlation between volume and quality.

It makes sense that the more times a doctor and a team perform a procedure, the better they get.

As I mentioned earlier, my hip replacement doctor does five hips each Monday and Tuesday morning. His outcomes are excellent. He has become very good at what he does.

Further, the best doctors attract the most patients, hence they do more volume. It is a virtuous circle. So volume is quality indicator number one but hardly sufficient.

Second, our health care specialists also dig into available quality information that comes from Medicare databases. We use two Web sites that glean consequential information from claims data, such as mortality and infection rates. They are Health Grades and Subimo, both for-profit companies. Aspirus, for example, ranks in the top 5 percent for heart hospitals in the Health Grade annual rankings.

Our HR department has a list of such high-value providers—those who give the best quality, price, and service—for many treatments. With help from Anthem, our network administrator, we have given grades of A, B, or C to the providers on our transparency site. It guides our co-workers to the best providers for value and away from the worst.

Let's be clear: there is *no* correlation between price and quality. It's counterintuitive, but, put simply, high price does not mean high quality, or vice versa. In fact, there is some evidence to suggest that good quality results in lower prices. (This is true in manufacturing and other sectors as well: companies with their acts together on quality often offer the best prices.)

Mandate Quality Disclosure

Our directory of best providers is helpful, but it could be a lot more complete and user-friendly. The problem could be solved for good if federal and state governments simply mandated transparency on quality and price.

Absent good quality information, patients are stuck with inadequate methods of finding the best doctor for procedures. They either talk to a nurse they know for guidance or they blindly follow their primary care doctor's recommendation.

I have made the pitch to politicians in Wisconsin that they should be consumer advocates who put quality information into the hands of consumer-patients. My contention is that citizens have an inalienable right to critical information affecting their health. But it never happens, probably because of the heavy-handed political influence of health care providers.

Normally, I don't like government mandates, but when it comes to consumer information, I favor them, much like those required in the markets for automobiles, houses, and mortgages.

In the interim, deep work is being done at several levels to use data mining to elicit quality results. For example, the Wisconsin Collaborative on Healthcare Quality (WCHQ) has been working with payers and most providers in the state on a voluntary basis to develop and publish usable statistics. WCHQ is a joint effort by providers, insurers, and payers in the private sector. So far, most of the findings deal with process inputs, such as whether an aspirin or beta blocker is delivered within thirty minutes of a heart attack after a patient arrives at a hospital. But WCHQ recently published three quality and cost comparisons on heart operation outcomes, which is where Aspirus and one other Wisconsin hospital scored at the top of a 100-point quality scale. Its ratings are available online at www.wchq.org.

The challenge for the collaborative is to collect more metrics on outcomes: Did the patient die? Did the patient need a repeat procedure? Did the new hip work?

Some additional outcomes are being added, such as blood test data for diabetics under care in a system. Both the A1c blood test and LDL cholesterol are tracked.

And it is displaying outcomes and charges across Wisconsin hospitals for treatment of pneumonia.

Next up should be inclusion of data from the Society of Thoracic Surgeons (STS) on heart procedures.

This is all excellent progress toward full transparency.

The collaborative's work will be helped by the new Wisconsin Health Information Office, to which insurers are sending their common data. Similar initiatives need to happen all over the country, and they need to happen now. Consumers and businesses who are footing a large chunk of the bill need the information.

More quality data exists than is commonly thought or known. There are quality comparisons in specialty fields, such as the STS metrics. There are internal metrics at different health care systems that are used for continuous improvement and error reduction. There are "tissue committees" that do post-mortems on operations.

Unfortunately, almost none of this information is released to the public. In this void, Serigraph has been searching for Centers of Value that are willing to divulge their track records on quality.

Aspirus published its metrics from STS, though the society must not have been happy about the public use of the data for competitive comparisons. For instance, Aspirus rates higher than St. Luke's, the high-profile Milwaukee heart hospital owned by Aurora Health. Aurora, the biggest health system in Wisconsin with twenty-five thousand employees, is one system that doesn't submit its hospital data to WCHQ. It opts for opacity with the exception of its physician clinic data, proving it can be transparent where it wants to be.

Aspirus does a respectable five hundred heart procedures per year. And because the Aspirus team outshines its competitors with objective quality data, Serigraph recommends co-workers make the three-hour drive when medical circumstances allow.

As a bonus, its prices are about 40 percent lower than Milwaukee prices. Further, through BridgeHealth, the brokerage firm, Aspirus now offers fixed or bundled pricing for heart procedures. We now know what our costs will be up front. One reason that Aspirus can take the risk of fixed prices is that it has less variation and fewer negative outcomes. In quality lingo, it has fewer defects. In this case, a by-product of consistency in quality outcomes is better pricing and bundled pricing.

S.C. Johnson, the huge consumer products company with products like Raid and Pledge, has long used a center of excellence model for joint replacements, heart procedures, and back surgeries to steer its people. The company, based in Racine, Wisconsin, selects three nearby centers for each of the three types of procedures. Its selection has been based on quality alone.

The company sends its staff doctors to audit the candidate facilities and then steers Johnson employees to those high-quality centers. Quality, not price, determines Johnson's choices. That company doubles the out-of-pocket maximum if employees choose to go elsewhere. Serigraph appropriated the concept of steering employees to centers of excellence from S.C. Johnson. We use the term Centers of Value, as we seek not only quality but price and service, too.

The important lesson is that you can dig out quality information if you are determined. The challenge for Serigraph and other payers is to insist on a more rigorous, user-friendly display of quality information. Consumers deserve to know this information so it can be used routinely in health care decisions.

Aspirus agrees. Its information package states: "We're all about transparency. This message must get to the consumer."

If businesses insisted that all health systems followed suit, better quality, better health outcomes, and better prices would surely follow. Their costs would drop.

Name_____

Address_____ Date_____

℞ TAKE-AWAYS ON ELUSIVE QUALITY

☑ Check volumes of procedures before hiring a doctor or health facility.

☑ Ask providers for their quality statistics.

☑ Steer employees to Centers of Value that divulge quality ratings.

☑ Push legislators to pass laws that mandate transparency on quality.

☑ Tap into Web sites that offer quality information.

MD_____

Signature_____

10

To Reform:
Educate, Communicate,
Hyper-Communicate

L AURIE KIRSCH opened the envelope containing her annual health scorecard after taking Serigraph's required mini-physical. She was chagrined to see her BMI (body mass index) flashed a red alert. Although her other health factors rated green and good to go, the BMI score put her on notice that she was up a few pounds beyond healthy limits.

She read the enclosed material about the dangers of being overweight, and, unlike many Americans, took the warning to heart. She made an appointment with Tammy Ertl, the company's on-site nurse practitioner. They sat down, talked, and came up with a plan.

Such attention to chronic conditions should be screamingly obvious (though it took me a while to figure it out). It's basic and should be noted again that you can't manage health costs without managing health. And you can't get people to manage their health without a large dose of education.

The communication programs of payers, health systems, and insurers are often inert. The messages usually reside on a passive Web site or in a brochure. They are there if someone wants to go find them. But to be effective, messages have to be more than just informational. They need an active, personal touch.

Our health coaches get directly involved. They get out on the floor to improve ergonomics. They meet co-workers face-to-face, including the third-shift workers once a month. It's a high-touch approach.

Because Laurie had access to her full health information and the education process, she got the connection between a healthy lifestyle, staying out of the hospital, and containing the health bill for herself and the company. She and Tammy devised a diet and exercise regimen, and she started shedding pounds. She feels great. She looks great. She is healthier.

The intense communication and coaching effort paid off for her, but it will also pay off in the long run for the company and other plan members who pay for the same pool of costs.

The wide range of negative health effects from carrying too much weight are well-known. It's beyond debate. But, for some reason, that piece of behavior change is the most difficult to bring about. Hence, there has to be an extra dosage of education and coaching.

Communicating with Co-workers

Serigraph has long had a philosophy of hyper-communication with its stakeholders, especially its co-workers. We have run an open-book company on our finances and business plans for two decades. That includes profit and loss statements and the company's balance sheet. We share all but the most sensitive information.

We have used every communication device known to man to stay in touch with co-workers: quarterly meetings for all co-workers on all three shifts, bulletin boards, an intranet site for company matters, a monthly CEO newsletter, regular department meetings, and mailings. So why would we not consistently address in all these venues our third-biggest area of cost—health care? We do. It is one of the main communication topics. Most quarterly meetings feature a health topic.

As discussed earlier in this book, a powerful communication device is our MedSave Web page, where we offer transparency on prices of procedures, as well as the best A-B-C quality ratings we can determine. In Wisconsin, such quality and efficiency comparisons are just starting to become available.

In addition, we publish a monthly newsletter on health issues by me as chairman (see Exhibit 10-1). It has been delivered as an e-mail, and a hard copy is posted on bulletin boards.

Every month, our on-site medical staff holds two "lunch and learns" on health-related topics. Our on-site provider publishes a monthly newsletter that is sent out via e-mail to employees, and hard copies are placed in the lunchrooms for those employees without e-mail access at work (see Exhibit 10–2).

Annually, our health care team reviews health appraisals with co-workers. Those face-to-face meetings with the health coaches are mandatory, like the assessments themselves, and help them earn points in our "Free Days" wellness program.

Anytime there is a major health concern, such as the "swine flu," we do a concerted communication program for employees through flyers, postings, e-mail, and face-to-face meetings to discuss how to deal with the incidence of the disease at home, as well as at work.

EXHIBIT 10-1

Chairman's Health Care Update
By: John Torinus Jr.
March 2010

ObamaCare – Little Impact at Serigraph—Despite all the hullabaloo in Congress, co-workers at Serigraph will see little change in their health care plan. Most of ObamaCare doesn't take effect until 2014, and it doesn't have much to do with health care delivery itself. It was mostly about insurance and access reform for people without insurance. Unfortunately, the president and Congress ducked the root problem in health care—rapidly rising costs. Premiums will continue to skyrocket, and it will get worse when the new provisions kick in. That means the company and co-workers will have to continue to innovate and make good decisions about our health and use of medical services. That's the only way we can keep a lid on the increases. Note: our average increase over the last six years has been only 2.8%, far below the national average of 8%.

ModernMed Signs 130—Dr. Mark Niedfeldt made his presentation to Serigraph co-workers for primary care, and he got 130 initial clients. Dr. Niedfeldt is a primary care doctor who specializes in sports medicine. He counts among his patients members of the Milwaukee Bucks, Milwaukee Wave, and Milwaukee Ballet. A good number of our co-workers liked what they saw. He operates out of Mequon but also will have office hours at Serigraph. The primary care is free to employees and their families. Serigraph is making the bet that the retainer we are paying Dr. Niedfeldt will be more than offset by eliminating office visits elsewhere, by better management of chronic disease, by better prevention, by fewer days in the hospital—by better health in general. Dr. Niedfeldt will work closely with our on-site clinic, where we already offer free medical, chiropractic, and dietetic services. We'll keep you posted on how this pilot program with ModernMed works.

Body Renovation a Good Buy—Most physical therapists charge sticker prices of $400 and $600 an hour, an outrageous range. But Body Renovation, which operates out of Grafton and Mequon, charges about $100 an hour, and they do really good work. The head of the firm, Rick Wagner, has a master's degree in physical therapy from the University of Wisconsin–Madison. Body Renovation is able to offer reasonable prices, because it keeps its overhead low, unlike

EXHIBIT 10-1 (continued)

the big health care systems that have huge overheads. You can save yourself and the company a lot of money by directing your physical therapy treatments to this excellent facility. Net prices are about $90 per hour.

Generic Drugs Still Free—Remember that Serigraph makes drugs free to co-workers if they are generic and purchased at Walgreens, Walmart, or Target. Those three retailers offer a long list of generic drugs for $1 a week. It is such a good deal that Serigraph wants to encourage its people to purchase there. That led us to the decision to reimburse that $1 per week, meaning that the drugs are completely free to co-workers.

Serigraph Way Under US Average—Our costs for 2009 came in at $6,648 per employee, well below the national average of about $8,659. Management and co-workers are managing these costs together to our mutual benefit. While we have an increase in our premiums for 2010, based on 2009 medical charges, it is only the third time in seven years that we have had an increase. The company is doing a better job at controlling health cost inflation than just about any other company in the country. For co-workers, it is a win all the way around.

Second Opinions Still Free—Remember: Before you decide on an elective surgery, check out the effectiveness of the procedure. As many as half of stent operations have been found to be unnecessary. Ditto for back surgeries. Serigraph has a policy of paying 100% for second opinions. Not all doctors are created equal. Some are very good; some aren't. Check them and their facilities out with our HR staff and with our on-site medical professionals. Get a free second opinion. Nothing is lost by doing so. I got five opinions before my hip surgery in 2005. Each surgeon had a different approach. I ended up with a very good surgeon.

EXHIBIT 10-2

INTERRA HEALTH™

InHealth™ News

Helping you live a healthy life to the fullest.

What's New InHealth

VOLUME 1, ISSUE 10

NOVEMBER 2009

Childhood Obesity and Parental Control

As a parent, it is natural to protect your child from harm. However, some of your family lifestyle habits could be harming your child's health. According to the CDC, between 1980 and 2006, childhood obesity rates have risen from 6.5% to 17%. Childhood obesity is the number one nutritional disorder in the U.S. and is caused by poor diet and physical inactivity.

Childhood obesity can lead to numerous health problems down the road. Obesity is associated with an increased risk of developing high blood pressure, blood sugar, and cholesterol levels, which are all risk factors for cardiovascular disease and type II diabetes. Obesity can also lead to asthma, sleep apnea, a weakened immune system, and social discrimination. Social discrimination can cause low self esteem and cause problems both socially and academically.

As a parent, it is your duty to instill in your child an active and healthy lifestyle. You are your child's primary role model and setting an example with healthy habits from birth will lead to a healthier child. If you, as a parent, are obese, inactive, and have a poor diet the chances of your child being obese and following in your footsteps rises significantly.

So, how can you reduce the risk of your child becoming obese?

•Encourage a healthy diet. Choose fresh fruits and vegetables and incorporate whole grains. Bake or broil instead of frying foods.

•Keep your serving portions in check. Children's portions are much smaller than adults.

•Develop an active family lifestyle. Go on family hikes or bike rides. Play yard games together.

•Encourage your children to be active with their peers. Support their involvement in sports.

•Limit sedentary activities like video games and watching television.

These small lifestyle changes can lead to a healthy life. For more information, try visiting mypyramid.gov or healthiergenerations.org.

www.cdc.gov, www.obesity.org

Controlling Your Portions

- **Keep seconds out of sight.** Serving meals family-style often leads to having unnecessary seconds.

- **Say yes to salads.** Salads that are full of veggies are not only nutritious, but they also help curb your appetite.

- **Know your trigger foods.** Buy snack foods in single serving sizes or divvy up full size packages into smaller, individual bags.

- **Breakdown your leftovers.** Separate food into small containers. This way you only reheat one leftover at a time.

- **Master mini meals.** Eating small meals every couple hours prevents overeating

- **Order a kid's size meal.** If you have fast food, order a kid's meal; it is the right portion for an adult and it saves you money.

weightloss.about.com

What we are getting this month...
Flu Shots!

What it is... The "flu shot" is a vaccine containing killed viruses that is given with a needle, usually in the arm. It is approved for use in people older then six months. The best time to get vaccinated is September - January. Outbreaks tend to peak in January.

What it does... About two weeks after getting vaccinated, antibodies providing protection against the influenza virus infection develop in the body.

Side effects... The viruses in the flu shots are killed (inactivated), so you cannot get the flu from a flu shot. Serious side effects are rare. Some people experience soreness, redness, or swelling at the injection site, or a low grade fever.

www.cdc.gov

Reminder!

Check your medical records or ask your doctor if you are up-to-date on your immunizations. Getting vaccinated helps your body develop immunity to a number of diseases.

www.healthpopull.com

"Time and health are two precious assets we don't recognize and appreciate until they have been depleted."
-Denis Waitley

Shelf Life for Coffee

To ensure your coffee always stays fresh and flavorful the best way to store it is in airtight, opaque container in your pantry. Make sure it is away from light, heat, and moisture. If you do not have an airtight container, close the bag tightly with a rubber band and store it in sealed plastic bag.

It is a common misconception that putting coffee in the freezer is the best way to store it. This is not true! The change in temperature creates moisture in the coffee which can alter the flavor of your favorite cup of joe.

It is ok to store whole beans in the freezer for up to a month as long as you are not taking it out during that time. When you do want to use the beans, let them thaw out before grinding them and make sure to use them within two weeks.

www.realsimple.com

Don't forget, points are updated the 6th of each month!
www.interrahealth.com

HIT THE TRAILS!

Fall is the perfect time of year to go outside and get some exercise! The weather has gotten cooler, the air feels crisp and refreshing, and the leaves are changing colors making the scenery absolutely beautiful. For outdoor activity, we recommend finding a park in your area that has trails that you can run or walk on.

One added benefit of running or walking on trails is that you burn about 10% more calories than exercising on pavement! The uneven terrain poses a new challenge for your muscles which causes you to burn more calories. Trails are also gentler on your joints and bones than the hard pavement.

If you are serious about trail running or walking, be sure to plan your route ahead of time. Websites such as TrailLink.com, Trails.com, or TrailRunner.com can help you find the right trail for you. Always be sure to stay safe by carrying your cell phone and ID while exercising on a trail. Going with a running buddy will also help keep you safe and motivated. So get outside, find a trail, enjoy the beautiful scenery, and burn a few more calories!

Health Magazine

Feel Full Longer!

Make snacks and meals count by choosing healthy foods that keep you feeling full longer. Foods that are dense with fiber, protein, and/or water, but low in calories will help you to feel full longer than foods that have little nutritional value and a lot of calories. Try incorporating the following foods into your diet.

Oatmeal- Look for the brand that has the most fiber and the least sugar.

Apples, raspberries, and pears- Most fruits are high in fiber. Eating the skins of fruits like apples and pears gives you an added fiber boost!

Melons and papaya- These fruits are water-dense. Even though they are the same size as other foods, they keep you feeling full longer and have less calories.

Almonds, walnuts, cashew, and pistachios- Not only are these full of healthy fats, but they are also full of fiber and protein. Remember a handful is all you need!

Low-fat popcorn- This whole grain is an excellent source of fiber.

Salads with fresh veggies and lean protein- A great way to start a meal so that you do not overeat.

Whole wheat products (cereal, crackers, pasta, bread)- Products made with whole wheat (as opposed to bleached and enriched white flour) are full of fiber.

Low-fat yogurt, cottage cheese, or string cheese- These are great sources of protein and an alternative to lean meats.

Brown rice- Another good example of a food high in fiber!

Click here to take the quiz! *(Available this month only!)*

Plan Changes Not Easy

When we made the conversion to a consumer-driven health plan in 2004, we knew it was going to be a major and complex decision for employees. We learned that many companies had flopped in the first year, falling short of desired enrollments. Part of their shortfall was insufficient incentives to make the switch from a low- to high-deductible plan. But another factor was a failure to adequately communicate.

Because communication has been in our DNA, we didn't make that mistake. We made the new health plan the centerpiece of the company-wide meetings a month before the conversion, and then we set up one-on-one meetings with every employee to go over his or her options.

One of the three options tracked our old plan, with a $300 deductible and 20 percent co-insurance. So the conversion to a high-deductible plan was voluntary.

The incentives to switch to a higher deductible were strong: a near elimination of the bi-monthly premium and a new personal health account. That, and the intense education about health care economics, carried the day. Two-thirds of our people saw the light and opted for the two high-deductible plans.

That percentage has risen in subsequent years as we have increased the incentives and deductible levels in all three of our plan options. The old low-deductible option is gone.

As with any major policy departure, we followed change management theory. We started by outlining the crisis. We made the case that the hyper-inflation in health costs threatened their personal solvency and the competitiveness of the company. We asserted that we either solved this challenge or job security was undermined.

Serigraph sells graphic parts to many industries, including the U.S. auto industry, so our co-workers are well aware of how bloated health costs were partly to blame for undermining the competitive postures of GM, Ford, Chrysler, Delphi, and Visteon. All but Ford ended up in bankruptcy court. Our message fell on fertile soil.

As with most advertising campaigns, one rollout of a message is not enough. Repetition rules. Our company continues a drumbeat of communication on health and health costs. The internal discussion points sound like this:

"Do you know what the local clinic tried to charge for a colonoscopy?"
"What's your cholesterol level?"
"Where's the best place to go for a hip replacement?"
"Do I really need a stent?"
"Let me tell you about the billing screwup from the hospital."

The more communication the better, so in 2010 we institutionalized that dialogue process by creating John's Healthcare Blog on SeriNet, our company's intranet site.

My newsletter is the basis for the blog, and Serigraph co-workers are invited to exchange insights about good deals in health care, the best doctors, and the most effective treatments.

Good Stuff on the Web

Fortunately, our communication/education program came along as a wealth of information became available on the Web. There are many good sites for medical information, such as www.mayoclinic.com, http://health.nih.gov, http://medlineplus.gov, www.webmd.com, and www.healthfinder.gov.

In one personal example, insights from a PBS program and what my wife and I found online saved me and the company tens of thousands of dollars. While checking out imaging centers of best value for our employees, I served as a guinea pig for a heart scan. I was surprised to learn I had some significant coronary blockage. My cardiologist decided I needed an angiogram to confirm or refute the findings from the less-precise CT scan.

I knew that balloon angioplasties and stents were almost automatic if the angiogram showed significant blockage. The puzzle was, I was asymptomatic, meaning I had no signs of heart discomfort or malfunction. I still competed, without distinction, in fifty-mile bike races and fifteen-mile cross-country ski races.

My wife had watched the public television report called "Stents and Sensibility" and learned there is no evidence that stents significantly reduce the risk of future heart attacks if there are no overt symptoms, like chest pain. She told me, "Don't do it."

I asked her to dig deeper for information on the Internet. Sure enough, five months earlier, a study endorsed by the American College of Cardiology showed that stent implementation in asymptomatic patients did not change outcomes or prevent future attacks.

I called the doctor's nurse the night before the procedure, and she became quite irritated with my questions about automatic insertion of stents during an angioplasty. I asked her if she had read the study. She hadn't. I insisted on talking to the cardiologist.

The doctor obliged by calling back that night, and he had read the study. Because I had no symptoms of heart failure, we agreed to just do the pictures, and then, after collaboration on the decision, to go back up my groin artery if necessary. As it turned out, the blockage in one of my main arteries was partly congenital—it had been there all my life, through many Marine Corps and sports exertions. There were other narrowed areas lower in the artery. They were caused by older plaque and not likely to let loose.

The cardiologist and I decided on a regimen of aspirin to thin the blood and a statin, but no stent. The company and I saved $35,000 by not stenting. That's what good information and communication can bring about.

Subsequent studies have indicated that the stent industry—that's what it is, an industry—is using the marvelous device twice as often as necessary. In 2006, Americans spent $14 billion on stent procedures.

Because stenting is so lucrative, and because it is little known that drug regimens are just as effective as stents for most heart cases, the number of stent operations remained roughly constant in the United States through 2008, at about one million per year. That's only a slight reduction from 2007, when the devastating study was released.

Insurance companies will try to force doctors to try drugs first before stenting, but only well-informed consumers can make a major dent in stent overuse.

Serigraph co-workers have been made fully aware of the ineffectiveness of stents for many cases of heart discomfort.

This kind of digging and improved decision-making led us to steer our health plan members to the reliable Web sites for information prior to procedures. Staff people in our Human Resources Department and our on-site nurses help them find the facts. Huge savings result.

Shared Decision Making

It is only a matter of time before states and insurance companies require doctors to engage in what is known as informed or shared decision-making. Many ineffective back, stent, prostate, and other types of surgeries will be eliminated when that happens.

In that vein, Serigraph makes second opinions on elective procedures free. We want our co-workers to seek out comparative information and advice on expensive treatments. I got five opinions before my hip replacement. Each surgeon used a different method.

Dan Fellenz, a maintenance worker, got two opinions before his shoulder surgery.

Further, our on-site doctor is available to help with decisions about surgeries.

END-OF-LIFE DECISIONS

In one controversial communication arena, the company has put out information on end-of-life decisions. Those decisions have huge cost implications, and, as with all health care deliberations, we want our co-workers to be informed decision-makers. We brought in a medical ethicist from Lawrence University, and he outlined the pros and cons of what are called advanced directives. These documents instruct family members and medical providers on the kinds of protocols available to a person in his or her final days. We make the forms, which we get from Anthem, available to our co-workers.

We made no recommendations on what those end-of-life decisions should be. Some people want no heroic procedures on their deathbeds; others want every available method used. It is a very individual decision. The company neither wants nor has access to those private documents. We don't even know how many people have acted on the information.

But we believe clear directives at the end of life are a logical extension of the principles of consumer-driven health care. Informed decisions are the best decisions. They also can be a great comfort to family members surrounding a dying person.

There are economic aspects to these tough decisions, but the main issue is the dignity and needs of the terminal person.

A radio talk show entertainer criticized Serigraph for even bringing up the subject, bleating that we were only trying to save costs. He refused to put me on the air to explain our side of the story.

Nonetheless, we still believe strongly that it is appropriate communication and education to make such information and forms available. Remember that the costs of heroic medicine are borne not only by the company but also by the rest of the employees. Indeed, heroic expenditures could be viewed as selfish or even immoral if the treatments are almost certainly futile.

Gundersen Lutheran, a health system in La Crosse, Wisconsin, sets the bar high for communication on end-of-life decisions. Thanks to an education campaign, more than 90 percent of its patients have filed advanced directives.

PERSONAL HEALTH RECORDS

Another communication and education tool is what's called personal health records (PHR). Some health care providers compile a patient's health data in a single file. They are private, open only to patient, doctor, and doctor's staff. Employers have no access.

One hospital system serving our market offers MyChartLink.com, a privacy-protected site that contains each employee's health records. It can also be used for setting up appointments and asking questions of their primary care doctor. It took far too long, but our co-workers can now e-mail their MDs.

Beyond PHRs, we are asking our providers to create an electronic medical record (EMR) for each of our people in their patient base. That would include all the PHR data, all digitized images, and more clinical information for the doctor's use. It's happening, but not fast enough. We need that communication vehicle as soon as possible. The best EMR systems (with all the privacy protections) prompt doctors to order timely tests and treatments. They catch problems like conflicting drug prescriptions. Several Wisconsin clinics are already 100 percent up and running with EMRs. Others aren't.

Our contracted doctor from ModernMed has a complete electronic record on every one of his patients.

Some day not too far away, that digital management and communication tool will carry the person's genetic make-up, which in turn will allow what is called "personalized medicine." As with other medical records, privacy must be paramount. But this advance will mean treatment plans that are customized to individuals. Bring it on!

Once that happens, collaboration will be even more in play between doctor and patient. The dynamics in my stent story will become commonplace. One result will be better quality of care and the related lowering of costs.

Most employees want to be responsible for their family's health and health costs. They want to manage that part of their lives. They want the latest information. Employers and providers have to respond by communicating intelligently and incessantly, by giving them all the information they need and deserve. Indeed, we hyper-communicate.

In 2012, Serigraph will encapsulate its communication in a Health Report Card for every employee and spouse. In addition to a health snapshot, it will lay out goals for the coming year, mutually signed by the individual and his or her primary care doctor. It will be updated every year. It will get people thinking about forward health planning, just as they look at retirement financial planning. They are learning that good health is a financial asset.

Name_____

Address_____ Date_____

℞ TAKE-AWAYS ON COMMUNICATION

☑ Health improvement and cost containment won't happen without education and good information.

☑ Don't just communicate—hyper-communicate on health matters.

☑ Transparency on costs and quality is imperative.

☑ New Web-based tools offering medical information help immensely. Educate your people on how to use them.

☑ Insist that providers make available personal health records and operate with electronic medical records.

☑ Urge employees to share decision making with their doctors.

☑ Educate employees about advanced directives.

MD_____

Signature_____

11

Silver Bullet for Better Value: Lean Disciplines That Transform

S ERIGRAPH OPERATING TEAMS—no slouches at quality and lean manufacturing disciplines—have made repeated benchmarking trips to Appleton, Wisconsin, to learn what ThedaCare, a four-hospital system with 5,500 employees, is doing to drive errors, infections, and waste out of its health care system.

Along with observers from all over the world, team members sit in on Friday morning "report outs," when cross-disciplinary teams of ThedaCare workers describe their latest projects that lift their performance to world-class levels. Every time, our people come back hugely impressed with ThedaCare's absolute commitment to finding breakthroughs in quality, service, and cost reduction.

There's an irony in this turnabout in who's learning from whom. John Toussaint, ThedaCare CEO, learned first about quality and lean disciplines from pioneers in the manufacturing world. He was one of the first to apply those principles to medicine. Now we are learning from him and his people.

Toussaint was a practicing physician in internal medicine and the business leader of ThedaCare, where he started eight companies, including a health insurance operation that sold for $40 million.

Most importantly, he is unafraid of necessary change. When a system is broken, as the economic and quality sides of medicine have been for decades, Toussaint goes looking for new business models.

His quest inside the medical world was similar to the path Serigraph was taking to come up with a better model on the payer side of the health care equation. So we ended up collaborating on a range of issues.

Toussaint's organization embraced quality measurements way ahead of other providers, beginning in the mid-1980s. Initially, defect rates ran between 50 and 250,000 per million opportunities. Those are not good numbers. But the metrics helped ThedaCare cut down on variation and errors in standard practices.

Still, he wasn't satisfied. Improvement wasn't moving fast enough in a still-broken system. Toussaint turned to the literature on the Toyota Production System for an even better model. He visited and benchmarked on lean companies like Ariens, an outdoor power equipment maker, HNI, a leading commercial furniture manufacturer, and Toyota itself.

If those companies could lead their industries, he reasoned, why wouldn't their obsession with lean disciplines work in medicine, too? Ironically, Toyota strayed from its core tenet of leanness in the last decade as it chased volume, and it is now paying the price with recalls, fixes, and market share retreat.

Toussaint launched ThedaCare into a lean journey in 2003. In the ensuing years, ThedaCare has delivered much higher value to its customers.

The voice of the customer always drives the improvement process. It's patient-centric, not doctor-centric. He pushed the organization to make continuous improvements in all three components of value—quality, service, and price. He demanded not only incremental improvements, but quantum leaps, as well. That's called discontinuous improvement.

As an example, its Appleton Medical Center has reduced the door-to-balloon time (the elapsed period from when a patient enters the hospital after a heart attack to an angioplasty in place) to thirty-seven minutes, the best in the country (see Exhibit 11–1). That's down from ninety-one minutes in 2005. Even the outlying hospitals in its system beat the national target of ninety minutes, using helicopters when necessary, to average seventy-five minutes.

As another example, Toussaint is now challenging his organization and other medical providers to get to "zero." He wants zero incidents of infections in his operating rooms and zero medication-reconciliation errors.

He was told his demand was impossible. But ThedaCare is getting there. It has had no medication errors for the past two years in one unit, and another has totally eliminated infections. That is a huge accomplishment, because errors in either area can kill. And errors are rampant in the overall medical world.

With those kinds of results, it became obvious that Serigraph should seek out lean medical enterprises in determining which to use as Centers of Value.

Further, there is a philosophical alignment. Since Serigraph uses lean disciplines rigorously in its own operations, we talk the same language.

ThedaCare is not alone in its war on infections. Partly in response to pressure from activist groups, including Consumers Union, 105 hospitals reported zero central line infections, the catheters into large veins.

The main solution is pristine sanitary procedures. We want our people to seek treatment for elective procedures at those high-quality facilities, even though the drive to get there may be longer.

EXHIBIT 11-1

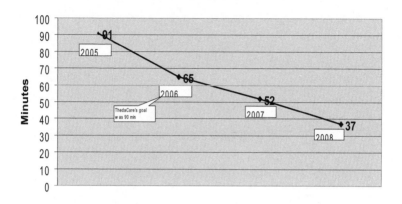

ThedaCare Door to Balloon 2006-2008

ThedaCare is also at zero for mortality in isolated coronary bypass surgeries (see Exhibit 11–2).

Indeed, ThedaCare's results have been so impressive that I tried to get Toussaint to set up a clinic in our market, but it was just outside his strategic geographical area. As a second-best solution, we are pushing our current providers to get more serious about their lean commitments.

In lean theory and practice, all processes and activities start with the voice of the customer and so it is at ThedaCare. A care coordinator, usually a nurse, meets the patient/customer on admission and becomes the quarterback directing the action from beginning to end of treatment.

If it's a knee injury, a sports medicine doctor is called in and quickly orders up the necessary tests. He gets the injured

EXHIBIT 11-2

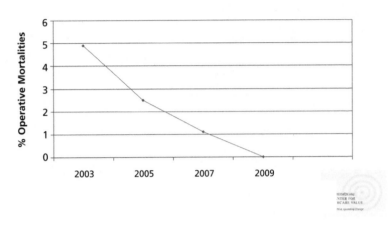

Isolated CABG Mortality

person in front of the orthopedic surgeon within a couple of hours, but only if it's necessary. If surgery is required, it is set as early as the next morning if the patient desires. It's smooth, efficient, and patient-friendly. Money is saved, because only necessary tests, visits, and work are done. The patient is fully informed and educated all the way through. Patient satisfaction numbers are off the charts.

Similarly, a woman coming in for a morning mammogram has her results by that afternoon. Anxious waiting is cut way down.

Most lab tests are accomplished at the front end of visits to a ThedaCare doctor, so more than three-quarters of patients have their results back before the end of the visit. That means some important things:

1. They usually don't have to come back for a follow-up visit.
2. They leave with an informed medical plan for whatever condition is being addressed.

That responsive service flows out of a corporate culture that involves every employee in continuous improvement of all facets of the enterprise. That cultural mindset looks at medical errors as defects in the process that need to be eliminated. In its five-year lean journey, Toussaint estimates that hundreds of thousands of potential errors have been prevented.

"The elimination of errors is a bottom-up exercise that needs to involve every single person in a rigorous way," said Toussaint.

Considered a prophet in his industry, Toussaint left his CEO post at ThedaCare to create the ThedaCare Center for Healthcare Value, an organization that promotes the lean philosophy in health care across the country. He has teamed up with the Lean Enterprise Institute.

"The solution to delivering better care isn't about having electronic health records, more insurance coverage, or more advanced technology," said Toussaint. "Unless we use lean thinking to fix the waste and errors first, all we're going to do is develop different ways to pay for and perpetuate a broken system."

The end result of his lean exercise showed up in 2008 quality statistics released by the Wisconsin Collaborative for Healthcare Quality (WCHQ). Its St. Mary's Hospital scored 100 on quality for three cardiac procedures.

Those kinds of outcomes should attract discriminating consumers. Competition between providers should be based on value, most importantly on quality, not on fancy campuses and expensive (but often unnecessary) equipment.

The lean approach also yields attractive prices. The WCHQ comparative ratings put prices at ThedaCare's major hospital at 30–40 percent below Milwaukee prices for the three heart procedures. That, along with the quality outcomes and the intimate service, makes traveling a little farther worth it.

The WCHQ Web site, www.wchq.org, includes a report that shows low prices and high quality often run together.

This is not to canonize Toussaint or to give five stars to ThedaCare across the board. Their system is not perfect. They acknowledge that their lean journey has only begun. But this is the kind of operation that payers and consumers should be looking for.

Further, systems like ThedaCare should be given big bonuses from payers, including public payers like Medicare and Medicaid, for keeping people well, for keeping them out of the hospital, and for eliminating errors.

Here are some other tell-tale results from ThedaCare's lean journey:

- Its pilot program for collaborative care pulls together a team of a doctor, nurse, medical assistant, and pharmacist for inpatient treatments. That method has reduced prescription reconciliation errors from an average of a little less than one per day per patient to zero. It is the standard for care for its new inpatient tower.
- Its clinic in Kimberly, Wisconsin, has most lab tests back to the doctor in fifteen minutes.
- If a patient calls in and needs to see a doctor that same day, a revamped scheduling system makes that happen 89 percent of the time.

The Lean Approach

For any company that has fully adopted lean principles, none of these results at ThedaCare come as a surprise. Lean is a profound system of change for the positive.

Learning from early adopters like Toyota and ThedaCare, Serigraph started its lean journey in 2005. We have reduced mountains of waste. As one example, we reduced our inventory from $16 million to $6 million. Lean disciplines turned $10 million in stored parts to $10 million in cash.

I have spent a half century in factories, from machine operator to management, and have used most of the innovations that have come along: quality circles, time-based manufacturing, constraint theory, synchronous manufacturing, quick-response manufacturing, and Six Sigma.

None of them work nearly as well as lean methods, which pull all those concepts together.

Lean is top-down and bottom-up at the same time. It uses simple problem-solving techniques and sophisticated statistical tools in tandem. It gives multidisciplinary teams the necessary time to figure out the voice of the customer and track down root problems before seeking answers. It puts enduring fixes into place in the present tense. Lean works.

You have to see first-hand to understand just how different and how much better the ThedaCare operation is from the management jumble that is the norm in the rest of medicine. Most hospitals are a cacophony of disorganization.

So why hasn't this powerful managerial philosophy been put to work more broadly in the medical world? There are many reasons, but the absence of market pressures from discriminating consumers is at the heart of it.

Payers like Serigraph, including insurers and their purchasing agents, need to push harder to move health care organizations off the status quo on quality and price.

Lots of organizations, including some hospital systems, talk the lean talk. I call it "lean light." But going "lean heavy" takes an enormous commitment at all levels of an organization. Only a handful of health providers have made the full leap.

That's too bad. We are all poorer and less healthy as a result. In lean lies one of several major answers for combating the hyper-inflation in costs and prices that plague the health industry.

A monumental irony in all of this is that ThedaCare is punished on its top line because of its effectiveness. If ThedaCare gets a patient out of the hospital in a day less than its competitor, it doesn't get rewarded. Under the bizarre pricing systems and discharge policies set by Medicare and followed by health insurers, it loses a day's hospital charge—typically in the $2,000 range.

Similarly, if ThedaCare keeps a person out of the hospital, it's the same story; it loses revenue.

If it eliminates a medical error, and therefore a repeat procedure—a redo—it loses revenue. Perversely, hospital systems get more revenue for fixing their own mistakes. That never happens in any other sector of the economy. In my world of manufacturing, defects, mistakes, or missed delivery dates mean penalties imposed by customers—the exact opposite from health care.

Because the federal government and health insurers pay largely for procedures, that's what they get—lots of procedures, lots of line items. It's like the old piece-rate systems that factories abandoned decades ago. Piece rates juiced up production, but they hurt quality.

The equivalent in today's medicine is the short, hurried office visit. The truncated visits run the pricing meter but fall short on service and quality. There is only enough time to address an immediate health symptom and little time for proactive health management.

Helen Zak, a Lean Enterprise Institute spokeswoman, noted, "Compared to traditional mass producers, lean producers typically require half the human effort, half the manufacturing space and capital investment for a given amount of capacity, half the engineering hours to develop a new product in half the time, while making a wider variety of products at lower volumes with many fewer defects."

"Imagine the results that similar improvements could bring in health care," Toussaint added.

A handful of other providers have also taken lean seriously, including the Cleveland Clinic, one of the world's leading cardiac centers. It has a team of fifty who lead its employees into continuous improvement projects. As an example, it displays patient waiting times in departments to keep the pressure on to value customer time with great attention.

Gundersen Clinic hired a chief financial officer from manufacturing, and he, in turn, hired a team of engineers to drive waste out of its operations with lean and Six Sigma disciplines.

There are glacial movements at the federal level to pay for value. There are ten Medicare pilots, for instance, including one at the Marshfield Clinic in Wisconsin to reward quality and keep people out of the hospital. Marshfield has earned large bonuses for proactive medicine. The pilots for more intelligent payments have saved millions of dollars, but, unfortunately, they have drawn little attention as a basis for real reform.

The lean players need to be winners. If they aren't, we're in for a lot more hyper-inflation in health costs.

Name_____

Address_____ Date_____

℞ TAKE-AWAYS ON LEAN DISCIPLINES FOR BETTER VALUE

☑ Seek out lean providers of health care and send your health care business there whenever possible.

☑ Insist on all three components of value: service, quality, and price.

☑ Push for changes in the archaic procedure-by-procedure pricing system.

☑ High value lean providers deserve more pay, not less.

☑ Set the bar at zero for infections and medication errors.

☑ Refuse to pay for redos or fixing mistakes.

MD_____

Signature_____

12

GENERICS, LOSS LEADERS PROVIDE LEVERAGE ON DRUG COSTS

ALICE NIXON has a black-belt in pharmaceuticals shopping. Because she was on a high-deductible insurance policy, she called retailers in her community to find the best deals. Invariably, she found huge variations in prices for the same drugs.

She and her husband, who retired as an independent sales representative for Serigraph, do most of their aggressive purchasing online with Costco, which they find to be 20–25 percent cheaper than any other retailer. Their pills are delivered by mail with no postage charge.

They are a perfect example of how consumerism can help to create a marketplace and bring down overall costs of health care, but there are other examples too.

When Walmart, Target, and Walgreen's decided to make generic drugs a loss leader, Serigraph jumped all over the offer. We couldn't believe they would sell dozens of generic drugs for $1 a week. Our first instinct was to question the offer; it looked too good to be true. We guessed that the charge to employees of $1 a week, or $4 for a thirty-day prescription, might be right but that there would be a significant balance charged to the company.

But, no, the $1 charge was the total charge—a better deal than our already aggressive drug plan.

We strive to make health care as affordable as possible to our co-workers, while simultaneously saving money for the company. So we decided in short order to make those generics totally free to our people. They simply bring their bill from any of the three retail chains to our HR department, and we reimburse 100 percent. That, of course, creates a nice incentive to choose these cost-effective generics.

The co-workers save money; the company saves money. Not only are they buying generic drugs at bargain prices, they are not buying the much more costly branded pharmaceuticals.

This is just one method of applying aggressive purchasing techniques to the sourcing of health care. It is an example of engaging co-workers as active consumers, as agents in helping to manage the complex problem of hyper-inflation in health care. It is also an example of using marketplace dynamics to bring about deflation.

At the national level, adversaries argue about whether advances in pharmaceuticals raise or lower overall health costs. Critics of Big Pharma contend that marketing expenses outweigh research and development investments at drug companies. They maintain that the massive advertising campaigns for brand-name drugs drive demand where it doesn't need to go.

Spinmeisters hired by the pharmaceutical giants counter that drug therapies, though costly, are less expensive overall than more invasive treatments. Pills, they maintain, often trump the scalpel in areas like heart disease. Advertising, they say, is a form of education, a way of providing useful information for consumers.

Those big-time arguments need resolution. Bans or limits on advertising deserve debate. Clearly, some drugs are nonessential, almost recreational or aesthetic in purpose. We draw a managerial line on some of those.

SOME RESTRICTIONS IMPOSED

For instance, Serigraph pays for only one blue pill per week for enhancement of sexual performance. We don't pay for baldness drugs. We cover drugs for smoking cessation, but only for two attempts at quitting. These are counter-measures to the incessant hype for those products.

Another knotty national issue is patent life for new drugs. It can take twelve years and a billion dollars to develop a new drug. With patents lasting seventeen years, drug companies don't have that many years to get a return on their development investment. That short-lived protection drives up prices in the short term. So does the necessary but rigorous drug testing required by the Food and Drug Administration before allowing a drug to be sold in the marketplace.

Meanwhile, at the ground level, payers like Serigraph have to deal with the cards currently dealt. We use pragmatic managerial techniques.

We, of course, let co-workers draw against their health accounts. It's their money, so they are as careful on drug purchases as for other treatments.

One proven management practice is to bid out a company's drug business through pharmacy benefit managers (PBMs) to obtain the best discounts off sticker prices. This has been standard practice for decades. Serigraph does it; so do many other payers, private and public.

Chasing discounts, though, is a standoff in the end. The payers, such as PBMs or health insurers, have assembled power on the buy side. But Big Pharma has consolidated on the sell side, and that offsets the buyer power. The argument that ever-bigger buyer pools produce big savings is weak, because there are diminishing returns on discounts beyond several thousand covered lives.

In other words, drug costs, which constitute 10–15 percent of a company's health care bill, can't be sufficiently controlled through competitive bidding.

THREE-TIER PRICING

A more effective management tool, and a proven one, is to deploy incentives and disincentives so members in a health plan strive to find the best value from their drug treatments. Many companies and their PBMs use a three-tier system of incentives.

In the first tier of Serigraph's plan, a typical one, low co-payments are the reward for buying generic versions of drugs. Co-workers pay either 20 percent of the drug price or a $5 minimum for a monthly regimen, whichever is higher (See Exhibit 12–1).

As an example, I use a generic, Lovastatin, instead of the costly Lipitor to knock down my cholesterol levels. My co-pay is only $5 for a thirty-day supply of the generic. The charge to the company for the balance of the bill is $11.17.

The low charge for employees in Tier One works very well at Serigraph. More than 90 percent of the prescriptions we cover are for generic drugs. Brand-name purchases are the exception.

We drive that percentage upward with a mail-order system that brings prices and co-pays down even more. My ninety-day supply for Lovastatin was only $10 through

PRESCRIPTION DRUG COVERAGE

Serigraph Inc. provides your medical and prescription drug coverage through Anthem and NextRx.

	RETAIL COPAYS	MAIL ORDER COPAYS
Generic:	20% of total cost with a minimum co-payment of $5	$10
Formulary Brand:	20% of the total cost with a minimum co-payment of $15	$35
Non-Formulary Brand:	30% of total cost with a minimum co-payment of $30	$75
Retail Day Supply:	30 days	90 days

More information regarding Maintenance Medications can be found below

After satisfaction of the $3,000 maximum out-of-pocket amount, generic, brand formulary and non-formulary prescription drugs will be covered at 100% for the remainder of that calendar year.

Mandatory Generic Substitution

The covered person must use generic drugs when they are available, otherwise the covered person must pay the difference between the generic drug cost and the brand-name drug cost, in addition to the generic co-payment amount. If the provider issuing the written prescription or the state in which the covered person resides does not allow generic substitution, the covered person shall be required to pay only the brand-name co-payment amount.

Maintenance Only at Mail Order: NextRx Standard Maintenance list is a comprehensive recommendation of medications utilized on a long-term or life-long basis. This list reflects the guidelines established by the Food and Drug Administration and drug manufacturers and promotes appropriate utilization using therapeutic effectiveness and safety as its main proponents. Drugs that are not considered Maintenance Medications are not eligible for mail order. NextRx will send notification if this program will affect any of the medications you are currently taking.

Quantity Limitations: NextRx clinical pharmacists have identified several non-maintenance high-cost medications that are not used daily but instead are used on an as-needed basis. The NextRx Quantity Limitations Program will adjust and manage the quantity of medication that a member can receive in a given time period, pursuant to FDA guidelines. NextRx will send notification if this program will affect any of the medications you are currently taking.

Specialty Pharmacy: NextRx Specialty Pharmacy program is designed to target high-cost injectable medications used for a specific category of conditions. An in-depth clinical review is done on a case-by-case basis by the on-staff pharmacists. NextRx Pharmacy then establishes a care team monitor and support each individual and his or her needs.

the mail. That was before Walgreen's, Target, and Walmart came along with their even-better deal.

In the second tier are branded drugs for which the PBMs have cut a good deal with the pharmaceutical companies. The co-insurance for the co-worker is 20 percent of total drug price with a $15 minimum.

For branded Lipitor, a higher-priced statin, in Tier Two, I would have paid $17.16 as my part of a monthly bill, and the company would have paid a balance of $68.63. Obviously, we are saving a lot of money by pushing the generics.

One response to the shift to generics was a new ad campaign for Lipitor. The ads promote the highly profitable Lipitor as the best statin for fighting cholesterol, but they never talk about cost.

Here's the contrast for a month's worth of drugs:

	Lovastatin (Generic)	Lipitor® (Branded)
Co-worker co-pay	$ 5.00	$17.16
Company share	$11.17	$68.63
Total	$16.17	$85.79

In just this one case, the annual savings to consumer and company by going generic can be $835.44. Multiply that savings by hundreds or thousands of users, and a company will experience major cost containment.

Some doctors will still prescribe a branded drug over a generic, and, indeed, that may be the best value for a particular patient. But, overall, generics work for most patients. My cholesterol is down to 179 from a high of 240 through diet, exercise, and Lovastatin. I and many other people don't need the more expensive Lipitor.

In Tier Three are the most expensive drugs. They are not included in Serigraph's recommended "formulary," our menu of pharmaceuticals with low prices and good results. The charge to employees in this tier is 30 percent with a minimum co-payment of $30. But we also require plan members to pay not only the minimum co-pay but also the difference between the price of an effective generic substitute and the brand-name drug.

Take Paxil, an antidepressant. A month's supply of this brand-name drug would cost $165, of which the patient would pay $49.50. The generic Paroxetine is far cheaper at $85, with the employee paying $8.

For thirty days of Prozac, another brand-name antidepressant, the cost is the $162.72, with the patient paying $161.08. The generic drug for depression, Fluoxetine, is a bargain at a total of $4.

In short, we penalize the use of expensive, branded drugs in favor of the effective generics. We do not feel that such a plan diminishes our coverage in any way.

High-Priced Drugs

A particular problem in the expensive tier is a whole range of newly discovered drugs that can be very effective against difficult diseases but very expensive. Some are "injectable" and can cost $1,200 per month. Our policy on those drugs is to cover them for the most part.

Glen Dorn, a truck driver for Serigraph, uses the injectable Enbrel to calm his rheumatoid arthritis. He self-injects the branded drug weekly, and it allows him to walk and perform his duties with much less pain. The drug works, and he can work. So it's a good deal for him and for the company, too.

But it isn't cheap. He pays $30 a month, but the company's cost is $1,570 per month. Ouch! That's nearly twenty grand a year.

There is no substitute drug, so Amgen, the pharmaceutical giant, has a lock on the market and can price with impunity. Surgical treatments are not a good option.

Should there be regulation of prices in such monopolistic situations? Probably, but don't hold your breath waiting for Congress to act.

As a practical matter, people using such exotic drugs have probably exceeded their out-of-pocket maximum. So it's 100 percent payment by the company in any case and free to the co-worker. Right now, there is no good answer for controlling the costs of these drugs, and the pharmaceutical companies can make a case that the high prices are necessary to recover their discovery costs.

Longer term, the drug patents will run out, opening the door to generic versions. In addition, volumes will rise if the drugs prove effective, eventually leading to lower price points.

At Serigraph, we do exercise oversight on what the doctors order. We want to know that the near-experimental regimens make sense. We use a consultant to approve inclusion of the drugs in our plan and to approve use for individual cases.

On the other end of the spectrum are some very effective over-the-counter (OTC) drugs. Prilosec OTC, for instance, is believed by many doctors and pharmacists to be just as effective as the highly advertised Nexium in treating acid reflux.

When we have such evidence, we grab the opportunity. We created an incentive by making Prilosec OTC completely free to our co-workers. Unfortunately, we haven't had many takers. But we keep working at such substitutions.

Early on, we experimented with mail-order drugs from Canada, which were a little cheaper for the same drugs than U.S. prices. It didn't prove to be enough of a savings, though, to go through the hassle of getting them across the border, so that initiative has mostly died out. So did the surrounding hullabaloo in Washington, D.C., from politicians taking aim at Big Pharma on the pricing differentials north and south of the border.

The secret, then, of keeping drug costs in line is to exploit the savings in the marketplace wherever they exist. At one-tenth of the company's tab for health care, drugs have to be managed as aggressively as the other nine-tenths of the bill.

Name_____

Address_____ Date_____

℞ TAKE-AWAYS
ON DRUG COSTS

☑ Use incentives wherever possible to exploit low-price opportunities in the marketplace for drugs.

☑ Use the proven three-tier system of purchasing drugs.

☑ Bid out your drug business but don't expect huge savings. It's a mature market.

☑ Make substitute over-the-counter and very low-price generic drugs free.

☑ Manage exotic drug discoveries for appropriate use.

☑ Take advantage of mail-order pharmacies that do a good job.

MD_____

Signature_____

13

BETTER MODEL
FOR DESPERATE
SMALL COMPANIES

A S SERIGRAPH WORKED ITS WAY through the innovations that allowed it to escape the hyper-inflationary trend in medicine, I tapped the expertise of three Wisconsin insurance brokers: Jon Rauser, Jim Mueller, and David Kracht. They buy health insurance for more than five hundred small businesses. Theirs is a tough assignment in the context of runaway premiums.

Their customers are subject to sharp, unpredictable jumps in insurance premiums.

The upward spikes have continued for decades. In 2010, premium hikes ranged from 15–25 percent for their small-business accounts. Jon, Jim, and David just shake their heads in frustration as they bring the bad news to their customers.

Further, many small business people ask me if Serigraph's success in managing costs can somehow be applied to their shops. The answer is yes, many of the innovations can be brought to bear for insured smaller employers.

Small employers pool together with many other employers in health plans to spread risk, but if just one employee in a small company becomes an expensive liability, premiums can skyrocket for that firm. That holds true in spite of various rate reforms at the state level.

The small firms have virtually no leverage on health care systems or insurers. They are too insignificant in the total marketplace to make a difference, and they are too small to self-insure like Serigraph does.

Without warning, insurance companies will increase rates as much as 50 percent in a single year if the small firm had a tough prior year for health costs. The insurers do it by reclassifying the risk level from preferred to standard or substandard. That move gets them around state limits on increases in a single year.

The end result is that small employers ask their brokers every couple years to move their business around to different insurers that might look at their group as a more attractive risk. The underwriting process is arduous. Each employee is required to fill out a detailed health questionnaire. And, in the end, it is difficult to move a policy.

Health insurance is such a nightmare for small companies that about 40 percent have opted out of coverage. Others have retreated to defined contribution plans, much like they have done with their retirement liabilities with a shift to 401(k) plans.

Going forward, companies with more than fifty employees will be forced under the new law to provide coverage or pay a fine. The fine is low, though, at $2,000 per employee. At $11,000 per employee on average in the country for health care costs, the $2,000 fine may seem like a bargain. The small firms, whether they have offered health care or not, will have a big decision to make on whether to offer a health care benefit.

Some small employers that use a lot of part-time help will structure their operations to keep employees below thirty hours a week, the level at which the fines or required coverage kick in.

Subsidies for small businesses providing coverage under ObamaCare will help, but we can only guess how many will keep or drop coverage when the mandate and fines take effect in 2014.

Because nothing in the new law reduces the underlying costs, premiums will keep rising, and that inflationary pain will weigh heavily on coverage decisions.

If a small business chooses to offer coverage, Rauser, Mueller, and Kracht offer some managerial steps to neutralize at least part of the escalation in premiums. They use some of the lessons learned in Serigraph's journey to a better business model.

Here is what these brokers recommend to their clients:

- **Buy a plan with a high deductible and co-insurance.** The premiums can be 20–60 percent lower than traditional plans with low deductibles and co-insurance. Almost all of their recent business has been in consumer-driven plans.
- **Facilitate the use of flexible spending accounts by employees.** Even though Congress dropped the maximum on the pre-tax accounts from $5,000 to $2,500, this is still a cost-effective approach.
- **Offset the high deductibles and co-insurance with a Health Reimbursement Account (HRA).** An HRA, an account for each employee that can be used for health expenditures, works better for small employers than an HSA, because no cash is required up front. Further, unlike HSAs, the HRA accounts can only be used for health care.
- **Hire a broker.** Though self-serving, a broker's expertise is necessary to wade through the dozens of health plan options offered by the big insurers. One national insurer, for instance, offers sixty-six different options for small businesses. It is almost indecipherable, especially for a small business person trying to do the multiple things every day that it takes to run a small enterprise. "Employers have

no clue as to what to select," said Rauser. Premiums are the same if you use a broker or go directly to the insurance company; the 3 percent to the brokers is paid by the seller. The government exchanges set to go into effect in 2014 will compete with the private brokers, but the private agencies think confusion in choices will persist or even get worse. They expect to still be in business.

- **Put your business out for bid every couple of years.** There is a lot of variation in the marketplace. In some swings in the business cycle, insurers are looking for new business and will offer a better price.

- **Be serious about prevention, wellness, and chronic disease management for your employees and their families.** Even if the plans offered by insurers and local health providers are mostly passive on programs to keep people healthy, make them active at your company. Keeping one person out of the hospital can greatly affect your premium levels in future years. Insurers look at claims data from previous years when they do their pricing. They adjust sharply upward for previous or ongoing large claims.

- **Pay for an annual mini-physical for your covered adults.** These exams allow employees to catch problems early, and medical problems are less costly when treated early. They can be done by nurse practitioners at a convenience clinic for not much money.

- **Look for an insurance plan that makes prevention tests free.** These include exams for breast, colon, cervical, and prostate cancers.

- **Encourage fitness for all employees.** The boss should set the example.

- **Look for a well-run primary care clinic to set up a medical home for each family.** Ideally, it would be one that has electronic medical records and can offer a personal health record for each person covered in your plan. Create incentives for your people to go there; it will reduce premiums over the long run, since large claims will be reduced.

- **Even if your premiums are set for the year, encourage your people to seek value.** If they go to a convenience clinic, for instance, their co-insurance and deductibles will be lower. The same is true if they go to a clinic during regular hours versus going to an emergency room. Your plan should include an out-of-pocket penalty for unnecessary ER use.

- **Encourage your people to look at the transparency Web site put out by your insurer to find the best values for price and quality.** Again, it will help them to drive down out-of-pocket costs, and it will help employees and companies earn better prices from insurers in future years. A high-quality provider will prevent medical errors and the costly aftermath of redos. Health providers charge to fix their own mistakes, but they shouldn't.

- **If you have a drug plan, use a three-tier or four-tier system that encourages the use of less expensive drugs.** These include generics and over-the-counter drugs. The plan should also discourage the use of expensive branded drugs, unless the doctor believes them necessary. Encourage plan members to use the loss leaders for generics at Costco, Walgreen's, Walmart and Target. At $1 a week, everyone wins.

The national health care debate at the turn of the decade paid some attention to small business. Beginning with the 2010 health care bill's passage, employers with fewer than ten employees can file for a tax credit of up to 35 percent of premium costs through 2013. Those interim credits phase out as an employer gets to fifty people or an average wage of $50,000. In 2014, credits for small firms that buy through government health exchanges will rise to 50 percent.

But if premiums continue to soar, and some economists think the new law pours fuel on the inflationary fire, small businesses may still choose to drop coverage.

What's really needed is a new business model. The standard insurance plans for small business just aren't working.

A convergence of the innovations and learnings in the private sector for the delivery of health care could accomplish a new business model. Insurance broker Rauser has introduced the package as "Ultimate Care."

In this new model, coverage at the base of the care spectrum is covered by a concierge or retainer-based primary care physician. A company can contract for one, ten, or twenty slots.

The top end of the care spectrum can be covered by a high deductible, say at $7,000 per person in a family. That would take care of the catastrophic events.

The uncovered middle between primary care and catastrophic could then be covered by a health account, either an HSA or HRA. The employee could be asked to share in any or all parts of this layered coverage.

Early quotes for this exquisite combination of care have been very promising—sharply lower, or at least low enough to offset the price of the primary care retainer for employees.

What's not to like? The business gets a reduction in health costs in year one. And it gets a robust delivery model in the years going forward. The model should help to keep people out of the hospital, the real way to reduce fundamental costs.

As for the employee, he or she gets lower, or at least stable, premiums, along with intimate primary care. The primary care portion can be offered free to employees. The plan member will benefit from a complete physical each year, integrated care in a medical home, serious chronic disease management, early detection of medical issues, and next day, unhurried appointments. The retainer doctor oversees treatments during hospitalizations.

You can even call or e-mail your doctor—what a novel idea!

The employees will have personal dollars in the game through ownership of their health accounts; it's their money, so the all-important consumer engagement will be at work on behaviors.

Finally, the retained doctor will help to steer or guide his/her patients to Centers of Value, where the most effective care is offered. Employees retain the right to choose.

It should be an effective model.

These kinds of innovations are needed to tame the hyper-inflation that plagues small businesses as they navigate the turbulence of health care economics. Federal subsidies are not enough.

Name_____

Address_____ Date_____

℞ TAKE-AWAYS FOR SMALL BUSINESS OPTIONS

- ☑ Adopt a consumer-driven plan so employees engage in cost and health management.

- ☑ Use new government tax credits for health care if company qualifies.

- ☑ Put emphasis on primary care to keep people well and out of expensive hospitals.

- ☑ Require annual mini-physicals to catch medical problems early, when they are curable and less costly.

- ☑ Teach your people to seek out value in the health care marketplace, namely quality and service, as well as good prices.

- ☑ Consider a primary care model, coupled with a catastrophic deductible and HRA.

MD_____

Signature_____

14

PRIVATE SECTOR REFORMS
TRUMP GOVERNMENT
EFFORTS

T HOUSANDS, perhaps hundreds of thousands, of
people in health care, now the largest industry in
the nation at more than 18 percent of the economy,
are working on various reforms of the system. Collectively,
they are making astounding strides on the medical side
of health care, including making many cancers treatable
versus palliative, allowing people with creaky joints to be

mobile again, and enabling people with major handicaps to lead useful lives.

A majority of the medical advances in the world are American advances, and there are many more to come, such as medicine personalized to each person's genetic makeup, the growth from stem cells of new organs, and the development of drugs that will treat Alzheimer's, Parkinson's, addictions, and other afflictions. These will happen because the researchers at our great medical institutions are closing in on breakthroughs in science. And they will happen in the lifetimes of most people.

There are also some major advances in the management of the delivery of health care, innovations such as electronic medical records, the elimination of infections in some operating rooms, and round-the-clock, electronically monitored intensive care units.

Yet all these advances in medicine, in technology, and in systems have not paid off on the economic side of medicine. Costs, prices, and the resulting insurance premiums remain wildly out of control. Insured businesses experienced double-digit premium hikes in 2010. Those staggering increases have driven more and more companies out of health care as a benefit; more than 40 percent of businesses now don't provide care.

With the national average at nearly $11,000 in health costs per employee, it should come as no surprise that struggling companies continue to drop coverage. Their exodus compounds the nation's access problem.

For some Americans, the natural reaction to the hyper-inflation and lack of access is to look to the government and hand over the payment challenges to the taxpayer instead of the employer.

But the hard truth is that public employers and public health plans do a terrible job of managing the economic side of health care delivery.

Public sector programs have to satisfy many stakeholders, so they have a hard time bringing about reform or change. More often, they are pushed relentlessly by interest groups to broaden coverage.

The result is that government at all levels pays two to three times per employee what is paid by well-managed private payers. For instance, Milwaukee County was spending more than $20,000 per employee annually on health care in 2008, the Cedarburg School District was at $24,000, and even a fairly well-managed Wisconsin State employee plan ran more than $15,000. In contrast, Serigraph was then running at $6,839, and we offer a full benefit plan.

The health law signed by President Obama in early 2010 was not, by nearly everyone's estimation, really health *care* reform but instead health *insurance* reform and access expansion. The underlying cost structures of health delivery in America went largely untouched.

A number of pilot programs were included in the new law, and some of those may some day change the way health care is delivered. But the wheels of bureaucracy grind slowly, so it will be years before any successes are worked into how virtually insolvent programs like Medicaid and Medicare are managed.

Meanwhile, the galloping cost, price, and premium trend lines will continue to point sharply upward. Indeed, most insurance companies are expecting to see premium increases accelerate because of ObamaCare. Just what we need—more fuel on the inflation fire.

It doesn't have to be that way. The innovations and reforms being put to work in the private sector are readily available to public and private payers alike.

There is no reason why a poor person on Medicaid, for instance, couldn't be given a health account of several thousand dollars, accompanied by reasonable deductibles and co-insurance. That would instantly put an end to many of the abuses plaguing Medicaid, such as recipients calling 911 and getting an expensive ambulance ride to an expensive emergency room for a sore throat or simple headache.

Don't think that example is an exaggeration. It happens every day in emergency rooms across the country. A friend who is an ER doctor quit because she just couldn't stand it any more. Another said emergency room physicians are often treated with disrespect, which often happens when people receive free care.

Similar abuses are endemic to other public welfare programs administered at the state or national level. Responsibility suffers when it's other people's money—taxpayers' money.

In contrast, I cannot remember a co-worker at Serigraph *ever* ripping off our system.

If a person in an entitlement program would pay something out of his own pocket, or even out of an account in his name that is provided to him, those kinds of abuses would be greatly mitigated.

Inevitably, because the financial pain will become so high for governments and taxpayers, there will be an imperative to figure out how to foot the bill. Government at all levels will have to deal with the cost of care that Congress inadequately addressed in 2010.

The federal government may be forced to set a maximum annual budget for health care, much as Canada does, which could lead to care rationing. Or it will have to raise more taxes to pay for the unaddressed inflation.

The better solution would be to learn from the reforms and innovations that have been deployed in the private sector.

Here are some hard-earned lessons in the private sector that, applied broadly, could produce savings to pay for the broader access, rescue government budgets, and bend the inflationary trend line downward. These proven tactics should drive what happens in both private and public sectors:

- **Change Who Pays**—Follow the lead of more than one-half of private companies, including most hospitals and health insurers, by changing who pays. Instead of third-party insurers or governments making virtually all payments, thus immunizing people from the economics, let the consumers pay directly for routine health care. With consumer dollars in the game, behavior changes, and consumerism and marketplace dynamics take hold. Use tax breaks or subsidies where necessary to give the consumers a hand in buying insurance and creating personal health accounts. Activate individual responsibility.

- **Restructure Payment System**—Instead of piecework payment by procedure, make payments for complete treatments. Bundle charges into one sum so consumers can understand what they are buying. Serigraph has negotiated some bundled prices, so it can be done. Year-to-year rate hikes could then easily be tracked.

- **Pay Bonuses for Good Outcomes**—The Marshfield Clinic in Wisconsin earned bonuses from the federal government in 2007 and 2008 for keeping Medicare patients out of the hospital. The clinic was rewarded for delivering high-quality results. Once people enter a hospital, the meter on costs starts running wildly, so pay incentives to keep them out. Otherwise, hospital systems will continue to be tempted to look at prevention as revenue losers.

- **Make Prevention Free**—Leading private companies are emphasizing good health. So they charge zero for mammograms, Pap tests, PSA tests, and even colonoscopies. They put low prices on primary care visits, such as $6 at QuadGraphics and $20 or free at Serigraph.

- **Flip the Pyramid of Care**—The health care system must revolve around primary care doctors, not specialists. The high-priced specialists should be called only after primary care providers, such as nurses, nurse practitioners, physician's assistants, and general practitioners, have done what they can for a patient. Public plans pay specialists much more than primary providers, just the opposite of what is needed. Create incentives, like loan forgiveness, to encourage medical students to go into primary care. Provide primary care at the work site, where possible, or in convenient clinics. Hire a retainer doctor to deliver exquisite primary care. Create a medical home for every plan member.

- **Lead with Lean**—Health care providers must adopt lean disciplines. They must follow the examples of the Cleveland Clinic and ThedaCare, where millions of dollars of waste and hundreds of thousands of potential errors have been eliminated. ThedaCare's prices are sharply lower than those of fat providers. The Wisconsin government subsidizes lean experts who consult with the state's manufacturers. Why not health systems?

- **Require Mini-Physicals Annually**—Health-risk assessments, adopted by many private companies at a relatively inexpensive charge, should be required annually. They are effective in catching high-risk situations needing immediate attention, in identifying chronic diseases, in convincing people to change lifestyles, in setting a platform for health coaching, and in allowing payers to measure and manage their overall health costs. Full annual physicals would be even better.

■ **Make Price and Quality Transparent**—People have an inalienable right to patient-friendly information on quality and real prices. Outcomes like infection rates of hospitals and doctors are slowly becoming available, but must be made widely and immediately public. Governments could mandate such information. As a start, they could easily publish their own price lists of what they pay. Payers, private and public, could require quality audits in the absence of forthcoming data. Transparency should apply not to sticker prices but to discounted, bundled prices that are understandable to the average citizen. Present pricing is a thick fog.

■ **Attack Chronic Diseases in Medical Homes**—Since 80–90 percent of health costs tie back to chronic diseases, those diseases have to be managed aggressively and proactively. The present fix-when-broken approach is backward and passive. Diabetes can be controlled; obesity can be mitigated; hypertension can be managed; depression can be treated. Payers and providers must set up systems to make sure that every at-risk citizen is surrounded by the people and tools necessary to ward off tragic outcomes. Accessible electronic health records are one such tool. Providers, insurers, and most payers have been paying lip service to this area of opportunity. Intelligent management and systemic care of chronic diseases must supersede episodic treatment. The most effective place to deliver such systematic care is in a medical home at the primary care level.

■ **Tilt to Generic Drugs**—The expiration of patents on many major drugs has led to the introduction of a huge variety of generic pharmaceuticals, and companies and governments can take advantage of their vastly lower prices by putting in tiered incentives to drive consumer/employees toward those excellent deals. Drugs can be made free to employees if the deals are advantageous enough.

Of the $2.5 trillion spent on health care in the United States, roughly half is spent by the private sector and half by government payers. Increasingly, private payers are adopting serious reforms on the economic side of medicine. For example, more than 50 percent of companies now offer high-deductible plans. Many use tiered incentives to encourage the use of generic drugs. Most have prevention and wellness programs. The result has been containment of the hyper-inflation that once gripped those companies.

As an example, costs dropped 22 percent at Bucyrus International in the year after it adopted a consumer-driven plan. Its union concurred in the decision and there have been no grievances about the new plan. The company and union achieved what amounts to cost deflation at a local level. Combined, many such ground-level victories have undoubtedly contributed to an aggregate cooling in the volcanic cost increases in health care. While still high, and well above the country's general inflation rates of 2–3 percent, health cost increases in recent years have averaged in the 6–8 percent range, down from the annual double-digit surges during the 1990s and early into this decade. Of course, that overall percentage includes federal health plans that use price controls to limit increases.

The general level of inflation in health care would decrease more if public payers would join in the movement away from traditional plans based on low premiums, low deductibles, and co-insurance, if they would manage health aggressively, and if they would insist on better performance from medical providers.

Most debilitating to effective cost management is the unwillingness of public administrators to engage public employees as partners, as mini-managers of the system, as responsible consumers, and as responsive public servants. Instead, they deploy top-down, paternalistic systems that keep public employees in a state of passive entitlement.

The same holds true for the major entitlement programs, Medicare and Medicaid. When people hit sixty-five, they move from being zealous consumers to a much less concerned and heavy user of care.

The economic fallout of non-engagement is horrendous. Medicare is projected to go into the red in 2017. Medicaid is busting state budgets across the country and the new health law will only add to the budget burden. School districts pay more than $20,000 per employee for health care and are headed to where health costs exceed base pay. Local budgets are strained to the breaking point by bloated health costs.

The inattention to available health care economies results in a crowding out of necessary public spending on education, infrastructure, and even public safety. School districts, for example, are laying off teachers across the country instead of managing swollen, under-managed benefit costs.

That sorry outcome is all so unnecessary. There are literally hundreds of billions of dollars to be saved if public organizations will become learning organizations—if they will learn from best practices in the private sector and, in some rare cases, the public sector.

They have to learn to manage, not just disperse funds.

As outlined earlier, Bob Ziegelbauer, the county executive with an MBA, knocked premiums down 40 percent in Manitowoc County, Wisconsin, after he benchmarked on reforms in the private sector. Everybody came out ahead, including the county's employees and taxpayers.

Invariably, members in the consumer-driven health plans report a high level of satisfaction. They like being in control of some of the health care dollars. They like lots of choices. They like having better information. They like it when their employers invest in their health. They do a better job on prevention and wellness.

Political leaders may have tackled the access problem. Now they need to solve the cost challenge and related quality issues.

Government health care reforms have focused on how to pay for a bloated system rather than on how to fundamentally reform it. That failure to adopt successful, proven private sector reforms is a road to government bankruptcy.

Our leaders need to build on the three platforms for fundamental transformation and reform of the U.S. health care sector:

- **Individual Responsibility.** We need to engage every U.S. citizen as an individual actor in managing his or her own health and health care costs. No system works without individual accountability. Proper incentives, education, and engagement of employees as consumers evoke that responsibility, and costs plummet.
- **Focus on Primary Care.** We need to put primary care back where it belongs as the major foundation of the delivery system. Intimate primary care greatly improves health and cuts costs by as much as one-third.
- **Centers of Value.** We need to promote the purchase of value-based health care in both private and public plans. Some providers offer significantly higher value than others. They should be rewarded with more business.

The U.S. president needs to personally visit the great innovators in the country—places like QuadMed, ThedaCare, Bucyrus International, KI, and the Gundersen Lutheran Clinic. He needs to touch, see, and hear what works to combat health care inflation.

He is welcome any time to talk with Serigraph co-workers about what works. They have tamed the beast.

Appendix:
2010 Benefits at a Glance

MEDICAL (ANTHEM)						
Medical Plan Bi-Weekly Premiums (April 1, 2010 – December 31, 2001)						
Medical Coverage Tier	$750	$750 Deductible Plan Smoker	$1,000 Deductible Plan Non-smoker	$1,000	$1,500	$1,500
Employee Only	$37	$39	$22	$24	$13	$15
Employee +	$72	$76	$42	$46	$24	$28
Employee +	$73	$78	$45	$51	$25	$31
Employee + Family	$100	$106	$49	$55	$33	$40

Medical Service	750 Deductible Plan		1000 Deductible Plan		1500 Deductible Plan	
	In-Network	Out-of-Network	In-Network	Out-of-Network	In-Network	Out-of-Network
Deductible Individual/ Family	$750 $2,250	$1,500 $4,500	$1,000 $3,000	$2,000 $6,000	$1,500 $4,500	$2,500 $6,500
Co-Insurance	75 percent	55 percent	70 percent	50 percent	70 percent	50 percent
Max Out-of-Pocket Coinsurance Individual/ Family	$2,500/ $5,500	$4,500/ $9,000	$3,000/ $6,000	$5,000/ $10,000	$4,500/ $6,500	$6,500/ $11,500
Max Out-of-Pocket Deductibles plus Coinsurance Individual/ Family	$3,250/ $7,250	$6,000/ $13,500	$4,000/ $9,000	$7,000/ $16,000	$6,000/ $11,000	$9,000/ $18,000
Office Visit	$20, then 100 percent up to $300/ visit max.	Subject to deductible and co-insurance	$20, then 100 percent up to $300/ visit max.	Subject to deductible and co-insurance	$20, then 100 percent up to $300/ visit max.	Subject to deductible and co-insurance
Wellness	$20 copay, then 100 percent up to $500/yr. max.	Subject to deductible and co-insurance	$20 copay, then 100 percent up to $500/yr. max.	Subject to deductible and co-insurance	$20 copay, then 100 percent up to $500/yr. max.	Subject to deductible and co-insurance
ModernMed						

All primary care services will be covered at 100 percent.
If you enroll in ModernMed, it will take the place of your $500 wellness benefit as described above.
* No co-pay, no deductibles, no coinsurance or out of pocket expense will apply.

*Services outside primary care may be subject to deductibles and coinsurance expenses

About Serigraph

SERIGRAPH EMPLOYS more than 1,500 people in plants in Wisconsin, Mexico, China, and India. It makes graphic parts for multinational customers like Ford, Honda, Nissan, Whirlpool, Coca-Cola, McDonald's, Arby's, Sony, Gillette, Ping, Kodak, and Nokia. It must operate at their extremely high standards for quality, price, service, and delivery.

Its four Wisconsin plants employ about 500 co-workers, all nonunion.

Typical products are the face of the instrument cluster in your car, the face of a control panel on your appliance, the graphics on your razor or golf clubs, and the in-store advertising in many quick-service restaurants.

Our prices are driven down every year by global competition. We live in a world of deflation, the opposite of the hyper-inflation in health care. Hence, our costs must be lowered every year through better management and practices.

Serigraph's manufacturing operations have achieved the following:

- ISO 9000, QSO 9000, and TS 16949, the highest international standards for operations
- ISO 14000, the highest international standard for environmental management systems
- Top quality ratings from customers like Whirlpool, Siemens, Maytag, Lorillard, Ping, Eastman Kodak, Mercury Marine, Delphi, De La Rue, and Kantus
- Recipient of the Wisconsin Forward Award, the state's equivalent of the national Malcolm Baldridge quality award

The company has been on a lean journey since 2005. It has employed Six Sigma quality tools for more than two decades.

Serigraph, which is self-insured, moved to a consumer-driven, employee-empowered health plan on January 1, 2004.